Felting Fashion

Felting Fashion

Creative and inspirational techniques for felt-makers

Lizzie Houghton

BATSFORD

First published in the UK in 2009 by
Batsford
10 Southcombe Street
London W14 0RA

An imprint of Anova Books Company Ltd

ISBN-13: 9781906388140

A CIP catalogue record for this book is available from the British Library.

15 14 13 12 10
10 9 8 7 6 5 4 3 2

Repro by Rival Colour Ltd, UK
Printed by Craft Print International Ltd, Singapore

This book can be ordered direct from the publisher at the website:
www.anovabooks.com, or try your local bookshop.

Distributed in the United States and Canada by Sterling Publishing Co.,
387 Park Avenue South, New York, NY 10016, USA

Contents

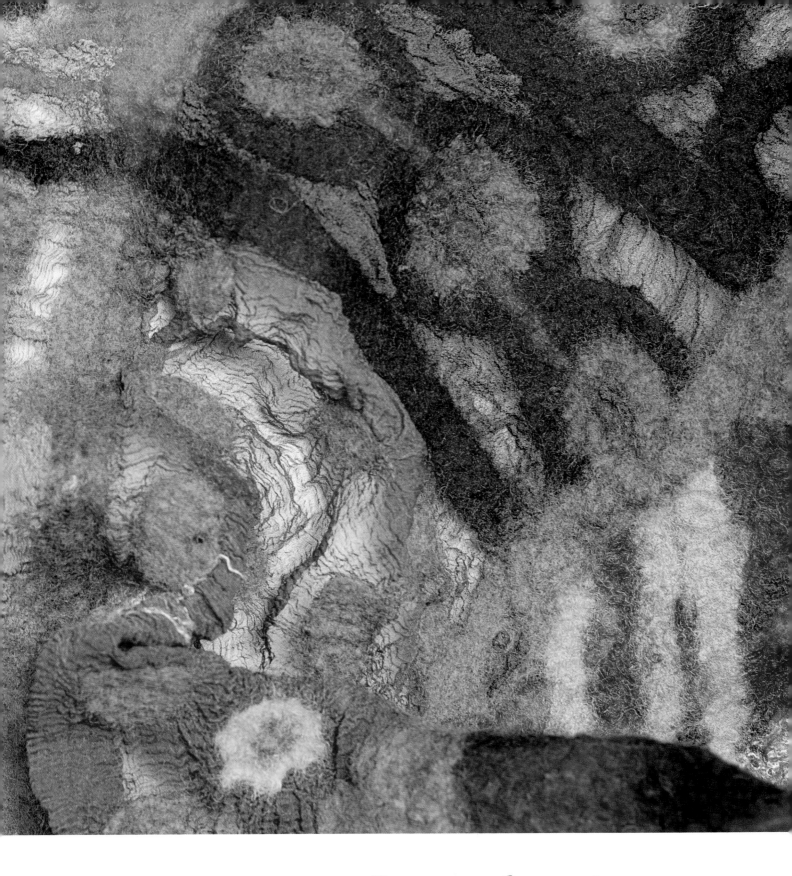

Introduction

Felt, the most ancient of all textiles, is a marvellous material. It can be shaped, moulded and sculpted and it repels water and dirt; for these reasons it has a long history of being used for clothing, headwear and footwear, too.

I originally trained as a fashion designer and had been working for years making clothing using embroidery and appliqué. It was when I was introduced to the techniques of making fine felt and clothing that I became hooked on feltmaking. Up until then, I had really only seen fairly thick felt and, thinking it would be rather suitable as a base for machine embroidery, made some rather lumpy stuff, taking instruction from a book. It was nice to stitch on, but I now know that it was quite badly made.

The first workshop that I attended was to make a coat. I am eternally grateful for having been allowed to join this class, because at that stage I was a real novice and I didn't really know how to lay the wool thinly and evenly. I also thought that it was necessary to use far more layers of wool.

The project was huge, and while making it I remember thinking that I would never make another one. However, I did keep working on it after the weekend course, and managed to finish it during the following week. Little did I realise that several years on I would be spending all my time making only felt garments and accessories.

Making seamless felt clothing does require a large amount of space, but the shapes can be quite simple and extra fullness can be shrunk away or even moulded on the body.

Nuno felt was a greater revelation to me. The fineness and fluidity was unlike anything I had ever seen before, and so suitable for making clothing. I have always loved colour, pattern and texture, and the textures possible using this technique know no bounds!

Opposite: nuno-felt jacket made on a base of patchwork silk chiffons. The jacket is worn upside down here for an alternative look.

About this book

All feltmakers will work in different ways. Although there are some elements of the process that are essential, the ways that they are put into practice are very varied. Although some methods may be more traditional, none are right or wrong. If it works – it works!

This book is intended to inspire feltmakers and encourage them to have a go at making a one-off individual garment that is a piece of wearable art. There are instructions on how to make small items for beginners, such as corsages and jewellery, and there are patterns and diagrams, with guidance, for making more ambitious projects for those who have more experience. Precise instructions are given for using different techniques and for creating exciting and interesting effects. The intention is not to show how to make an exact copy of the photographed items, but more how to select and design your own individual one. Various techniques and methods are described and if you have mastered one of them then you will be able to follow the guidelines and make a felted wearable, be it a brooch, a scarf, a hat or a jacket. With practice you will be able to make them all.

I am very grateful to those great feltmakers who have so generously provided images of their work. They have inspired me and the inclusion of their work allows the reader a glimpse into the world of international contemporary feltmakers.

Opposite: very fine nuno-felt jacket showing many textures where different weights of silk have been used. The jacket is reversible and is shown here with the silk fabric on the outside.

Inspiration

Much of my own inspiration comes from the natural world and other aspects of my surroundings also inspire me. A digital camera is a marvellous invention for me as it means I can capture everything I wish and it is not an extravagance to take as many photos as I like. I have mine with me most of the time. However, it does not mean that I consciously use all this inspiration directly in my work, just that I am absorbing colours, textures and shapes into my visual imagination.

I love flowers, the shape, colour and form of them, such as the minute patterns on petals and leaves, the odd dot of colour in the centre; the spotty petalled lily, stamens with brilliant orange chenille anthers dangling, carefully balanced on the end; checks, stripes and spots on fritillaries, foxgloves and delicate chiffon-like irises. Statuesque echiums, growing ridiculously tall and at strange angles; enormous aeoniums, rosettes of rich purple with acid-yellow flowers sprouting occasionally. The shapes and form of cacti and succulents, wonderful tree trunks and bark, covered with lichen and moss, and all the other plants to be found in sub-tropical gardens never fail to inspire. Beaches are a great source of fascination too: swirly and pearlescent shells with intricate patterns and textures; sea glass and stones in myriad colours and markings; rocks with strata and cracks resembling shibori dyeing, rockpools and glorious seaweeds with frills and contours that could have been made from nuno felt.

Inspiration can come from further afield too, from holidays to pictures in magazines and travel advertisements. Or it can come from the most unlikely places – Sunday markets, decaying buildings or shady side streets. There are exotic African, Asian and Mediterranean markets with their colourful fabric, flower and produce stalls; intriguing fruit and vegetables piled together or beautifully arranged, and fish with iridescent patterned skins. Also layers of flaking paint and rusty metal eroded after battling with the elements.

How I work

I have quite a strong visual imagination and when I am about to begin making a new garment, I think about it and 'see' it in my mind's eye before making diagrams with measurements that indicate how to cut the fabric or pattern. Then begins the fun part, and for me the most important part – selecting my colours. I like to have out on my worktable a variety of different qualities of fabrics in near and complementary colours. I believe that most colours can be used together in a mouth-watering way as long as the proportions are balanced. I spend a lot of time playing with colours in this way. There are no rules, only what works for you.

It would be fair to say that my clothing is created organically. I will already have decided on my base fabric and possibly the fibre colour, but the fabric that will be added for texture and embellishment will be chosen as I work. I love my garden when flowers freely seed into the gravel or unplanned crevices, and so when making felt it is the little unplanned 'surprises' that I find exciting. You won't often hear me say 'less is more' except, of course, when making fine nuno felt. I love to create a wonderful chaos of colour and texture; layer upon layer of silks and wool.

Above: nuno-felt jacket, showing shaping at the back. Silks and velvets have been laid into the wool during the making.

Equipment for feltmaking

The equipment for making felt is very inexpensive and easy to come by. Some of it you will probably already have at home.

Old towels are used to spread on the work surface to soak up the water, stop your work slipping and can be used to roll your felt in during the final stages.

Bubble-wrap with small bubbles is used to give the friction needed to felt the wool. A matchstick, bamboo or similar blind with the metal attachments removed can also be a useful piece of equipment, especially for large pieces of work. It can add extra friction, but I would recommend also using the bubble-wrap as the blind can be rather rough and will not give such a smooth finish. These blinds may often be found in charity shops.

An old-fashioned washboard is very useful too, as a finishing tool. The wool or when, making nuno felt, the fabric side, can be worked against the glass, steel or wood ridges to provide the friction needed to help with shrinking.

A rolling pin, a piece of dowel or a length of plastic foam pipe insulation is required. Ideally, the roller should be as long as your work. The foam pipe insulation is much lighter to use if you are working on a large scale. It is very cheap to buy from DIY shops, can be bought in one or two-metre (one or two-yard) lengths and can be cut with scissors.

Old net curtaining is sometimes used to place over the wool to prevent the fibres moving while being wet out (while water is being added).

Thin plastic dust-sheets, available from DIY shops in packs about 3.5 x 3.5m (12 x 12ft) square, or on a long roll, is used to help spread the water through the work and support the wool during the felting process.

A spray bottle, which can be a plastic milk bottle with holes punched in the lid, is used for wetting the fibres. Some felting suppliers now sell a plant mister, which has a bulb spray and a small rose at the top (shown on the previous page). This is becoming popular with feltmakers as the spray is fine and even and does not move the fibres. A plastic trigger-action plant spray tends to have too fine a spray and does not wet the fibres quickly enough, making it very hard work.

A bar of soap. Although any soap will work, some of the cosmetic soaps make too much lather so olive oil soap is best to use and kind to your hands, too. This dissolves in hot water, but may also be used as a bar to add soap to the felt (shown on the previous page). I usually put the soap in a jug and add hot water to dissolve some of it and pour the solution into a spray bottle. I then remove the bar to use separately.

Hand carders are used for blending fibres and mixing colours. They are flat wooden brushes, supplied as a pair, with hooked metal teeth and a handle (shown on the previous page). The wool fibres are placed on the teeth of one carder and gently brushed with the other one, the hooks pulling in opposite directions. You only need these if you wish to blend your own colours – they are not used in the felting processes described in this book.

Previous page: useful equipment for feltmaking includes hand carders, a spray bottle and a bar of soap.

Left: washboards, like this one, can be found in second-hand shops if you are lucky, or are available new from some fibre and felting suppliers (see page 126).

How to make felt

There are many different ways to make felt, but this is the way I do it. For most of the projects in this book I have used merino wool tops, unless otherwise stated. Tops is the raw fleece, washed, carded, combed and dyed, before being spun. Merino felts very easily and makes a fine, smooth felt, most suitable for clothing. It is very readily available in a huge number of lovely colours; blending gives many more colours and it will also dye very well.

Each individual fibre of the wool has little scales on it. When the wool becomes wet the scales open up and, to enable the wool to felt, the fibres must become tangled. The three essentials for this to happen are heat, moisture and friction. Soap, preferably unperfumed, is added to help with this process.

1 Put an old towel on your work surface and lay bubble-wrap on top with the bubbles facing upwards.
2 Divide the wool top lengthways to make it easier to handle. Pull out small tufts of fibre, holding it loosely near the end, and place down one side of the bubble-wrap, each piece of wool overlapping the previous one like roof tiles (see figure 1). Form rows across and down the bubble-wrap, with each one overlapping the one before. The felt is going to shrink by approximately 25–30 per cent in each direction, so consider the finished size when laying out the wool. There should be no gaps between the fibres. It is worth taking time in this first stage as the more even the wool, the smoother the felt will be.
3 Place a second layer of wool on top, in the same way, but at right angles to the first layer (see figure 2). This is so that when the scales open up they will be able to hook on to each other. Two layers are enough to make a fine, smooth felt, but for something stronger apply more layers. Pattern may be applied on top.

Opposite: this coat is made using the network-felt technique described later in the book (see pages 34–39).

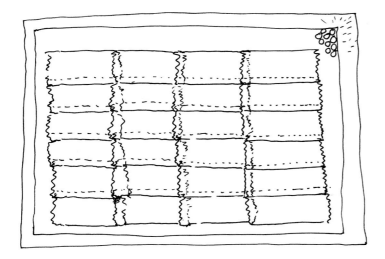

Figure 1: lay out the wool fibres, overlapping them like roof tiles.

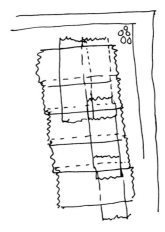

Figure 2: place the second layer of wool at right angles to the first and continue to lay out like roof tiles.

Above: back of nuno-felt jacket made using hand-dyed silk fabrics and fibres, showing the shaping at the waist.

4 Fill your sprinkler bottle with hot, soapy water. Some feltmakers like to put a piece of net curtain over the top before wetting the fleece to prevent the fibres moving, but the fibres do start to work through this and the net has to be removed, lifting the fibres. If your sprinkler has a fine spray the fibres will not move. Thoroughly wet the wool and spread the water by placing a piece of thin plastic sheeting over it. The fibres will stick to this, while you are working. Put water on to the plastic so that your hands will slide easily over the surface. Press down to remove the air and help the water to penetrate the fibres. It is possible to lift the wool gently with the plastic acting as a support, to check that it is completely wet, and if not, apply a little more water to the underneath.

5 Rub the surface of the plastic in a circular motion to begin the felting process. Turn the pre-felt over on the plastic ('pre-felt' is when the fibres have started to felt together but have not started to shrink). Using the plastic as a tool, turn the edges in a little to neaten them or, for a more natural, organic edge, gently draw the edges in towards the centre with your fingertips to thicken them. Turn back to the plastic-covered side and continue rubbing. Try pinching the fibres between your finger and thumb to see if they pull up, and when they no longer do you can start rolling, which is the 'fulling' process. This shrinks and thickens the felt.

6 Roll the felt tightly in the bubble-wrap around a rolling pin or dowel. Roll backwards and forwards for several minutes, unroll, make a quarter turn, and continue rolling. Repeat this until you have rolled in every direction. Remove the felt from the bubble-wrap and plastic. If the felt is to be used for only decorative purposes and will not receive much wear it may well be strong enough at this stage. However, for anything wearable it is important that it be very well felted so that it will be durable and not pill or become hairy. Immerse the felt in very hot water and, keeping the felt soapy, squeeze and roll in your hands. Further shrinking will take place by rolling it in the towel.

7 Finish the felt by rinsing out the soap in cold water. Re-shape and leave to dry.

Working with cords, spikes and balls

Cords

Cords are fun to make and can have many different uses, from shoelaces to necklaces, and from bag handles to fashion embellishments. They can be knotted, plaited, spiralled or joined at the ends to make loops. They may be made to be extremely thin or very thick and chunky. Different colours may be used for each layer and then they can be sliced through when dry to use as buttons or for jewellery. There are two ways to make cords:

Method 1

Take a length of wool tops and rub, while still dry, between the palms of your hands. Wet with soapy water and roll again on the bubble-wrap to wet through and form a long cord (see figure 1). Flatten another length of fleece and roll the cord in this, wetting as you work (see figure 2). Repeat this process until the cord reaches the desired thickness. Add hot water and continue rolling until the cord is very firm. Rinse and dry.

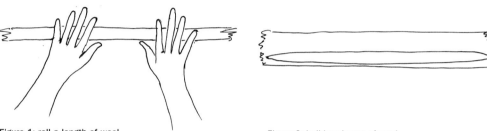

Figure 1: roll a length of wool tops while dry and then sprinkle with water.

Figure 2: build up layers of wool, rolling and wetting each time.

Method 2

Take a length of fibre and flatten it with soapy water. Using different colours, repeat this process to build up layers until you have a thick, flat strip (see figure 1). Roll this up all together and roll it until it is thick, firm and well-felted (see figure 2). When sliced across, the different colours will appear as a spiral.

Figure 1: build up layers of wool, wetting each layer.

Figure 2: roll tightly and continue felting until the cord is very firm.

Balls

Take a small pinch of fleece and roll it in a circular motion between your palms. Add another layer of wool and, wetting it a bit with soapy water, continue rolling, ensuring that the ends are tucked in. Wet and roll again, adding another layer of fleece. Continue with this method until the ball is the size you require. When fully felted the ball should be firm and be able to bounce a little. There are many uses for these bobbles. They may be embellished with beads and threaded to make a necklace or tiny bobbles could be stamens for a corsage, for example. They could be buttons or earrings, used either as they are or sliced in half, especially if layers of different colours have been used.

Figure 1: to attach a stalk or spike, spread out the 'roots'.

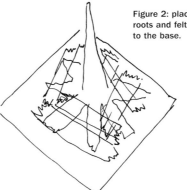

Figure 2: place fibre over the roots and felt to secure the stalk to the base.

Below: a bunch of stalks add an extra flamboyance to the crown of this hat made by Evelyn Refsahl.

Stalks and spikes

Make a spike or stalk by rolling in the same way as for making cords but, so that it can be felted into a base, leave the ends of the fleece dry to form a sort of root. Spread the dry wool out around the base and lay it on to the base felt where it is to be attached (see figure 1). Lay fleece over the dry felt in all directions (see figure 2). Wet it with soapy water. Make a hole in the thin plastic and pull the stalk through to stop it felting into the base felt. Work around the base so that it is firmly attached. Continue to felt it, making the end pointed, and then roll and finish the whole felt in the usual way.

If the stalk is to be attached to a flower then the dry end may be felted on to a pre-felted flower (see page 33). Several short spikes or long cords may be placed tightly together and used for embellishment, and the dry roots spread out together and anchored to the base (see page 30).

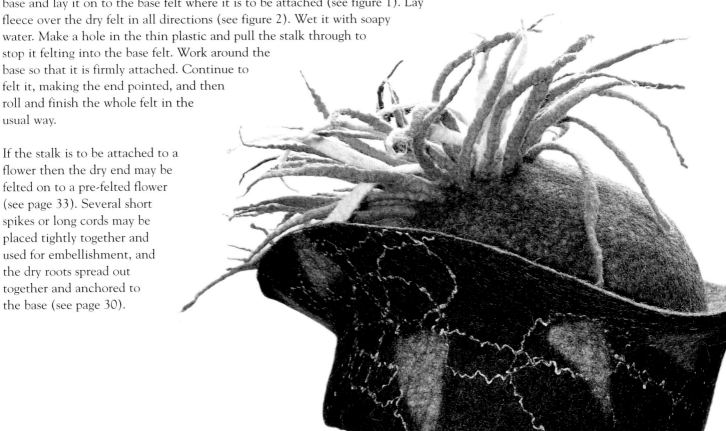

Making a spiky brooch

Make a dozen short stumpy spikes, or longer floppy ones, in a variety of colours, leaving dry roots at one end. Make a circle of pre-felt and spread the roots out, keeping the spikes close together (see figure 1). Add fleece over the roots to felt in the spikes and attach them to the background (see page 29). Make holes in the thin plastic and cover, pulling the spikes through. Work in and around the spikes to firmly felt them into the base. You can also continue to work the spikes by rolling them between your hands. Finish the felt and add a brooch pin to the back. For a different effect beads may be added by either threading them on to the spikes or by stitching them on to the base.

Figure 1: spread the dry roots of the spikes on to a circle of pre-felt.

Right: the spikes can be styled in different directions and beads added for further embellishment.

Making an exotic flower corsage

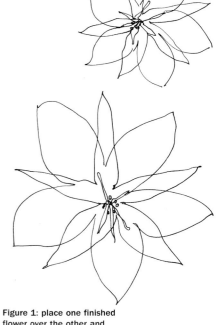

Lay out short lengths of wool tops in two flat flower shapes overlapping at the centre and bringing the wool to a point towards the ends of the petals. One of the flowers could be a little smaller if you wish (see figure 1). Place a few silk fibres over the wool, wet out and cover with plastic. Felt and finish. Sometimes the petals may become a little elongated during the felting process. Stretch them back to size and press with an iron. Dry flat.

Make some stamens by rolling tiny bits of wool into very fine cords, or alternatively use purchased stamens and thin coloured string, as shown below. To further embellish the flower, veins can be stitched into the petals either by hand or by machine. Place one finished flower over the other, staggering the petals, and stitch through the centre, adding a few stamens. Tiny felted balls could be stitched into the centre as an alternative. To make the flower more three-dimensional, pinch through the back of the two flowers and secure with a stitch or two. Attach a brooch pin to the back.

Figure 1: place one finished flower over the other and stagger the petals.

Left: the finished flower corsage.

Making a spiral flower corsage

This is a simple and very quick way to make a pretty corsage. The method can also be adapted to make clusters of flowers too. I often use all those little bits of wool that are left over from other projects, and blend them together to make softer colours. The corsages look prettiest if made very fine and silky. When you have had a practice you may like to make several at the same time.

Materials

- A selection of wool tops
- A few green tops
- A few silk fibres in white or colours

Method

1 Lay out the tops in a circle on the bubble-wrap, making two fine layers at right angles to each other (see figure 1).
2 Arrange the silk fibres thinly on top, remembering that they will not felt to themselves and need the wool to trap them, and cover with plastic sheeting. Placing your hand underneath, flip it over and apply silk fibres to this side too.
3 Wet with warm, soapy water. Cover the surface with thin plastic and wet the surface so that your hands will slide smoothly over the top. Work in a circular motion, making sure that the edges are felting together. Turn over now and again and work on the reverse.
4 At the pre-felt stage, when the fibres are starting to felt but not shrink, make a cut from the edge of the circle towards the centre. To make the flower a little more delicate, small holes may also be cut into the edges (see figure 2). These cut edges need to be sealed now so, using soap on your fingers, rub them gently on the bubble-wrap. Remember, holes get bigger with shrinkage, so don't overdo the size.
5 Continue to complete the shrinking in the usual way. Iron flat to bring out the beautiful sheen of the silk. Leave to dry.

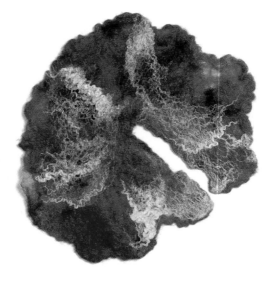

Figure 1: place two layers of wool in a circle at right angles to each other.

Figure 2: cut from the edge to the centre and make small slits near the outside edge.

Right: these could be used separately or together to form flower heads. Spiral one on top of the other or spiral separately and place side by side.

The stem

1 Make a green cord by rolling a length of around 20cm (8in) wool. Keeping the end fibres dry, for shaping a leaf, wet in soapy water and continue rolling, building up the layers until the desired thickness has been reached and the cord is firm and fully felted.

2 Now shape the end fibres, which have been left dry, into a leaf, adding a few more fibres if needed and maybe silk fibres also. Complete the felting.

Finishing

1 Twist the flower head into a spiral (see figure 3), and secure with a few discreet stitches around the base.

2 Attach the stem by folding the leaf around the base of the flower and hold in place with hidden stitches.

3 The petals of the corsage can be folded back to open out the flower.

4 A brooch pin may be attached to the flower head at the back.

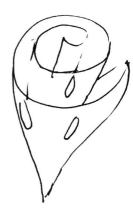

Figure 3: twist the flower head into a spiral and attach the stem.

Below: the finished corsage.

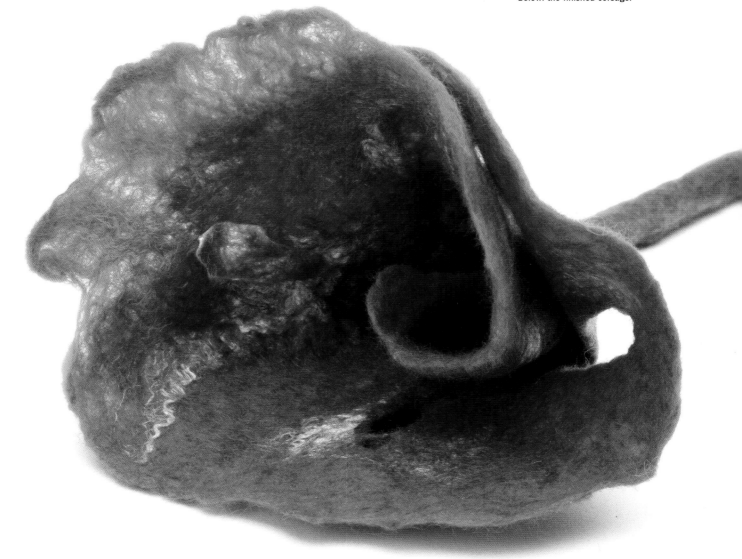

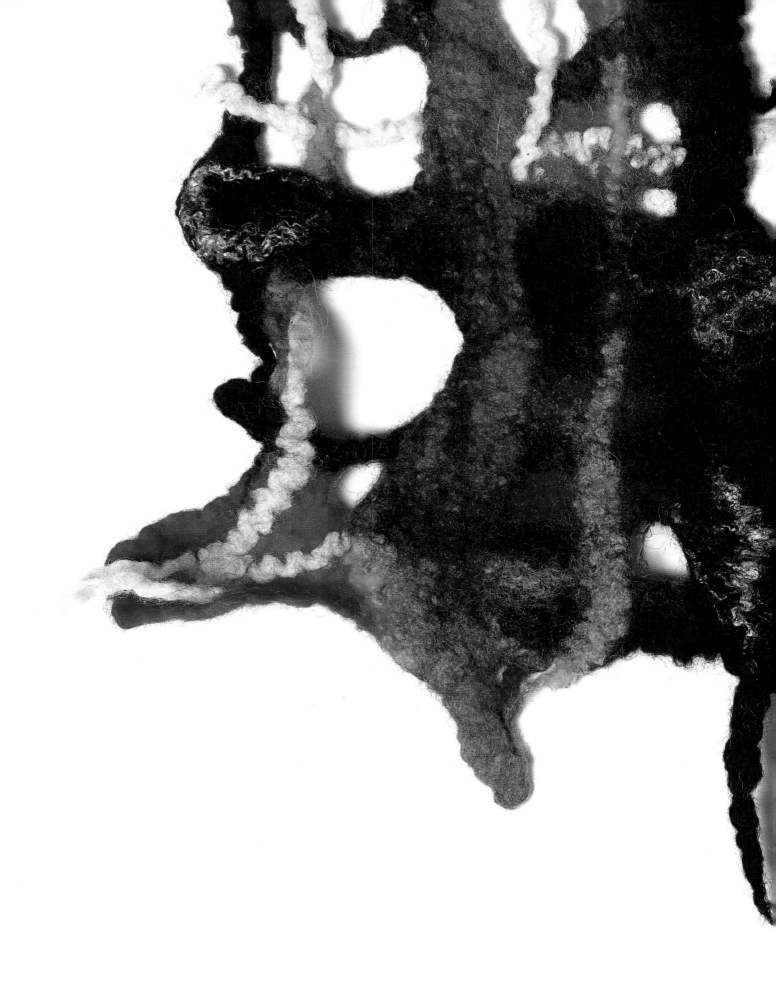

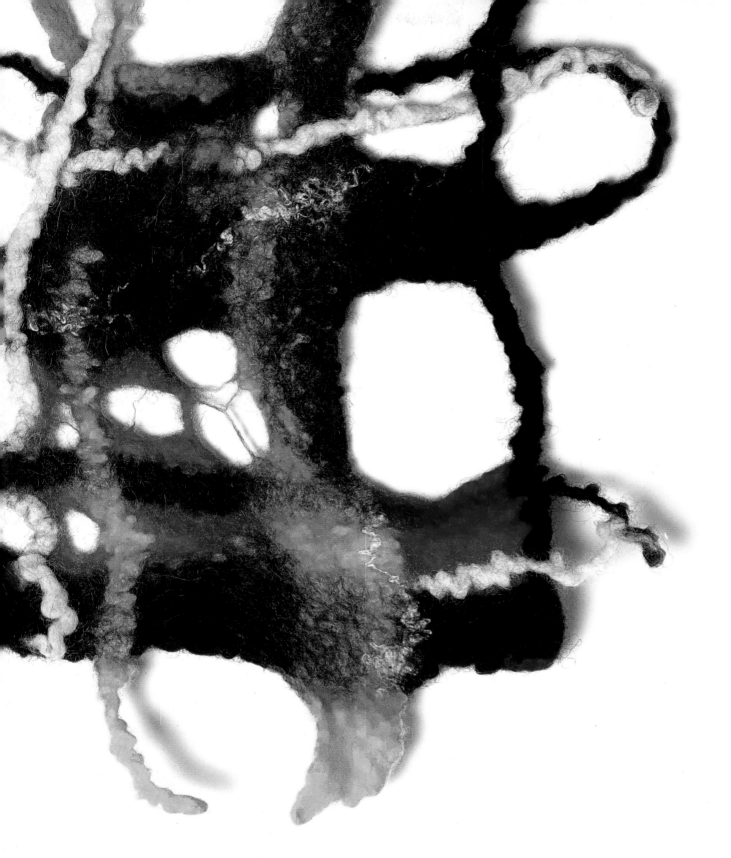

Working with network felt

Above: a network felt tunic made by Evelyn Refsahl.

The lovely thing about network felt, or felt lace as it is sometimes known, is its lightness in weight and look, although it is actually very strong. Because there are holes in it, it folds very easily around the neck and is therefore very suitable for making scarves. The felt is made by laying out the tops with spaces left in between them. The easiest way to start is by making a grid, either horizontally and vertically, or diagonally. Amazingly only one layer is necessary but of course, where the crossovers are, there will be two layers. When the double layers felt, the single ones will be pulled together and become narrower.

Making a network-felt scarf

To make a scarf, draw a rectangle approximately 2m x 40cm (2¼yd x 16in) on to the bubble-wrap. If you have decided to make a simple horizontal grid then lay a length of tops all around the drawing (see figure 1). If your lines of wool are fine, to begin with you will find that they get narrower and the holes will become larger. If the wool is thick when you lay it down, it may spread when wet and close the holes up a little. Keeping the lines parallel, lay the wool down the length of the scarf and then across. Wet out, cover with thin plastic sheeting and felt in the usual way. Lift the plastic and check that the lines are in the right place before continuing. When it is finished and rinsed, stretch and pull the scarf into shape before drying.

Make a diamond-patterned scarf by laying the wool diagonally, stopping at the lines on the bubble-wrap (see figure 2). Place the other rows at right angles. There will be a choice to be made at the edges – either the rows will meet and form chevrons or, if they are left separate, the edge will be fringed.

There is no rule to say that the rows are to be equidistant or running in the same direction. Try combining vertical lines with diagonal ones. Small pieces of chiffon could be placed over some of the spaces, but make sure that they are big enough to felt into the wool.

An alternative way to make a similar but different effect is to make a scarf with two fine layers of wool and at the pre-felt stage, or before the final shrinking, cut some slits and holes in the felt. As the felt is then finished with plenty of soap and some water, the edges will be sealed.

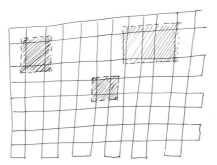

Figure 1: sample network felt layout showing a straight edge on one side and a fringed edge on the other. At this stage, chiffon may be placed over some of the spaces. Make sure that the fabric is big enough to felt into the grid on either side of the holes.

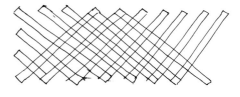

Figure 2: fibres laid in a diagonal grid and joined at the edges form chevrons.

Above: network felt embellished with different fabrics.

Left: in this sample, squares of chiffon have been placed over some of the holes and felted in.

Cobweb felt

Cobweb felt is deliciously fine and airy and when combined with silk fibres has a beautiful glossy appearance. To make a cobweb scarf, first draw out the size of the scarf on the bubble-wrap, allowing for shrinkage.

Lay out the wool fibres very finely, either by pulling out tufts, or by using one length of tops and spreading it widthways, making sure that there are no twists in the fibres. When it has been laid to the required length, allowing for shrinkage, spread a few very fine wisps of wool across the width. Silk fibres may be lightly scattered over or even silk hankies (several fine layers of silk cocoons spread out into a square shape). It is important that the silk fibres are trapped by the wool fibres, as they will not felt to themselves – therefore lay them on top before wetting the wool. Wet the felt, cover with plastic and begin to felt. Holes will appear in the felt, but that is part of its beauty. If the holes are too big then quickly put a few more fibres over before felting further as they may get bigger. Finish the felting by rolling and stretching into shape after rinsing.

Opposite: cobweb-felt scarf made using hand-dyed silk and wool fibres.

Using resists
and templates

Resists and templates

A resist is used to prevent layers of fibres from becoming entangled. It can be made from closely woven cotton, thin plastic (dust sheet), builders' plastic, bubble-wrap or plastic foam of the sort used under laminate flooring. I usually use thin plastic for a flat pocket, flap or layer and the foam underlay for anything that needs to be three-dimensional.

For special textures it would also be possible to use string or ribbon laid on to the surface of the wool. Fibres would then be laid over the top and felted. A narrow channel would be formed around whatever had been used, which then could be cut open. Make sure that your choice of resist will not be trapped by the fibres and become felted in.

A template is also a resist and the techniques described here for making hats and some of the jackets are made totally enclosing the template. A template is usually cut to the exact size plus shrinkage allowance of whatever three-dimensional item is to be made. The template material that you choose to use should be flexible and the foam underlay that I use also has a firm edge that helps to prevent 'ridges' forming around the edges. The wool fibres can be worked against the template, as you will be able to feel the edges through the layers of wool.

Above: close-up detail of a jacket showing a bag pocket, which has been made using a resist.

Using resists to create pockets

It is easy to make pockets that are integral to the garment you are making. I suggest you practise first by making sample pockets before incorporating them into your garment. The most difficult thing is to calculate the right place for them to be, when shrinkage is happening in each direction. However, when you have perfected these techniques it is possible to make more complex decorative three-dimensional ones.

1 Lay out the garment first, wet out and flatten the fibres using your usual method.
2 Cut a resist the size of the pocket you require plus an allowance for shrinkage. Use thin plastic that will lie flat on the surface of your garment. Cut the plastic longer than it needs to be so that it will protrude above the pocket.
3 Place the plastic resist in the position required and cover with wool fibres in two directions, extending over the sides to attach it to the garment, but making sure that it is not covered at the top (as shown in figure 1). Wet out and flatten.
4 Cover the complete garment with thin plastic and felt in the usual way. Check that the pocket has not moved position during the process. Work the top edge to neaten it, before the final shrinking.

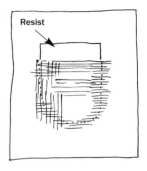

Figure 1: place the resist in the pocket position and cover with fibres in two directions.

Adding a flap

The main problem that occurs with adding flaps is that the flap may shrink away from the pocket, so make sure that you make it long enough to cover the top part of the pocket well.

1 Follow the process described above in steps 2 and 3.
2 Cut a piece of thin plastic that will extend beyond the pocket at the sides and position it over the top of the pocket, as close to the top as possible, so that it covers about a third of the pocket's height.
3 Lay the wool fibres over the top edge of the flap resist only, leaving the sides open, but ensuring that it will attach to the garment. Check that the flap will just cover the size of the pocket, but not extend too much at the sides (see figure 2).
4 Wet out and flatten. Proceed as in step 4 above, checking that the edges of the flap are felted well.

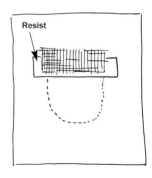

Figure 2: laying fibres over a resist to create a flap.

Making a pocket bag

This style of pocket is a little more bulky because it is three-dimensional, but when it is part of the design it looks rather interesting. The technique also lends itself to experimenting with other design features. The pocket is covered with the wool fibres at the beginning when the body of the garment is laid with wool. This style of pocket may also be made in the side seams by extending the template.

1 Cut a piece of the plastic foam for this pocket and tape it, with a hinge on each side, to the garment template. Don't forget to add shrinkage to the resist and calculate where the pocket is to be placed (see figure 1).

2 Lay out the wool on the garment and around the pocket area. Flatten the attached resist to lay wool on one side, overlapping the edges and paying particular attention to where it joins the main garment. Wet out this area and flatten (see figure 2).

3 Place a small piece of plastic on the garment at the base of the pocket (see figure 3) and fold the pocket over on top of it (see figure 4). Bring the wool over the edge of the pocket resist and place fibres on the uncovered side (see figure 5). Place thin plastic over the whole pocket area and felt garment in the usual way.

4 When finished and shrunk the pocket can be pushed through to the reverse of the garment and pressed if required.

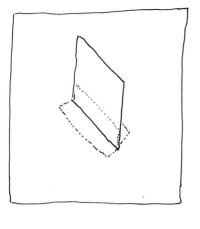

Figure 1: place the template for the pocket bag on the garment template. Using tape, stick it down with a hinge on both sides so that it can be flattened to either side while being made.

Figure 2: lay out the wool on the garment and on the pocket template, overlapping the edges.

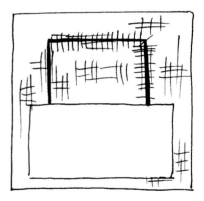

Figure 3: place the resist at the base of the pocket.

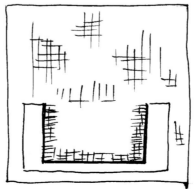

Figure 4: fold the pocket down over the template and bring the fibres over the edges.

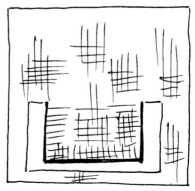

Figure 5: complete the pocket by laying wool over the uncovered side.

Making a pocket in the side of a garment

Calculate the size and the position of the pocket, allowing for shrinkage. Cut a template and tape it to the side of the garment template. The pocket could be cut all in one with the template, which would be easier. Cover the pocket section with the same thickness of fibres as on the main body of the garment. Complete all the felting together. When the garment is finished the pocket will be pushed to the inside.

Make a nuno-felt pocket separately, pre-felting and then stitching to the side seams before completing the garment. Push the pockets to the inside.

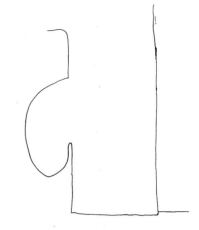

Pocket bag in the side of a garment.

Three-dimensional pockets

Interesting design details may be added by using this technique, though it can be a little tricky to work out. It is easiest to make the pocket in pre-felt before attaching it in place. Make it in paper first to work out which parts need resisting as you attach it to the garment. Make sure that it is securely felted to the garment, working around the joins.

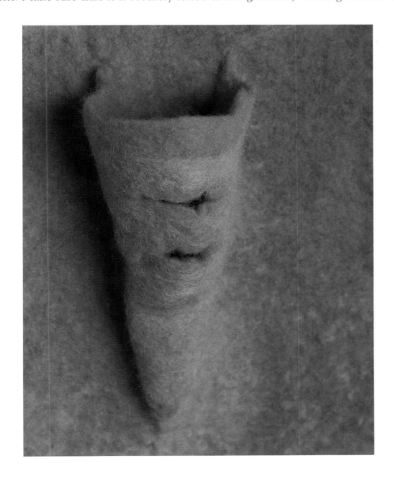

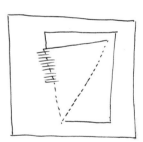

Make a pre-felt pocket and attach one side using a resist.

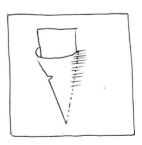

Keep the resist inside the pocket and felt the other side.

Left: funnel pocket. This V-shaped pocket has been slashed before finishing.

Using a resist to create a seamless item

1 Cut a resist or template to the desired shape, adding an allowance all round for shrinkage of approximately 25–30 per cent (make a felt sample first in your chosen fibres to enable a fairly accurate estimation to be made). Make the resist from either laminate flooring underlay from DIY stores, a piece of calico that has been washed, pliable plastic or bubble-wrap. Transparent plastic is useful if decorating your felt, as the design will be visible to repeat on the second side.

2 Lay down the towel with the bamboo mat on top if you are using one, and then a piece of bubble-wrap or thin plastic. The resist, or template, will go on top of this.

3 Lay out the fibres on the resist, making between three and six layers, depending on the item – for example, three layers for a hat, six for a strong bag or slippers. It is important that you remember to put the same number of layers on each side of the template. It is easier if you lay no more than two layers on each side before wetting out and turning over. This is so that you can make sure that the wool is pulled up against the template. Start by laying wool horizontally, overlapping the edges by about 1cm (⅜in) and make a second layer vertically, not overlapping the edges. Each layer should be fine and even with no gaps in between. Note that the first layer on each side will be the inside of the item you are making.

4 Sprinkle a liberal amount of soapy water into the centre and place the thin plastic sheeting over the top. Place one hand under the template and flip it over so that the template is now on top. Wet the edges of the template and then carefully fold in the fleece, using the thin plastic to help you pull the wool against the edges of the template. Make sure that the corners are not too bulky by spreading the wool a little further inwards. Lay wool horizontally but do not extend it right up to the edges. This would give too much bulk. The next vertical layer may extend 1cm (⅜in) over the edge. Wet in the centre, place thin plastic on top and turn back to the first side. Fold over the edges as before. The template should now be completely enclosed. Continue laying the wool until you have the required number of layers. When it is thoroughly wet you may apply any pattern, either in wool, appliqué or fabrics. Cover with plastic.

5 Wet the plastic and begin to massage the felt in from the edges all the way round. This is to prevent ridges forming. Fullness may form in the centre of the template, but you can ignore this as when you turn it over and begin the process on the reverse it will gradually shrink away. Continue working the edges only, until the wool has begun to fit closely to the template. Try the pinch test with your finger and thumb. When the fibres will not easily pull up you may start rolling.

6 Keeping the plastic in place, roll the felt up tightly in the bubble-wrap. Roll backwards and forwards for about five minutes. Unroll, check the felt, smoothing out if necessary, and turn it through 90 degrees. Re-roll and repeat the process until you have rolled in each direction and on each side. If the template is beginning to curl up inside, pull it to stretch and flatten it. It is the continual shrinking and stretching that strengthens the felt. Remove the plastic.

7 Carefully cut open the top of the felt for a bag and the bottom for a hat, through to the resist, to make the opening. Leaving the resist inside for a while, continue to work the

felt, smoothing out any ridges that are forming, by stretching and shrinking and by inserting your hand inside. Finish the cut edges of the item by rubbing with soapy hands against the bubble-wrap.

8 Turn the felt inside out and remove the resist. Make sure the item is well felted. Continue rolling. Using very hot water, throw the felt down on to the work surface to complete shrinkage. Rinse in cold water to remove all of the soap. Shape your item as required by stretching, and dry as you wish. You may like to press the felt with an iron and a damp cloth.

Finishing edges

Normally when making traditional felt, the edges will felt together during the making process. Where the felt has been made using an enclosed template and has been cut open then a little work will have to be done to seal those cut edges. Keeping the felt soapy, rub against the bubble-wrap until the rough edges have vanished. If you wish to have a decorative shaped edge then cut it before finishing.

Below: shell hat made on a template with silk fibres and velvet added to the surface.

Embellishment

Adding fabrics

The texture of wool felt is very matt and can look quite dull. However, with the addition of other fibres and fabrics it can be made much more vibrant. Make a selection of different qualities of fabrics in silk, cotton and rayon. You can use fabrics from your scrap bag or recycled scarves or clothing from a charity shop, and some synthetics. Choose colours that look pleasing together. Cut the fabrics to a similar shape and size, such as strips or squares.

Make two layers of fleece, and wet out with warm soapy water. Arrange the fabrics on top. Chiffons, georgettes and other fine fabrics made from natural fibres will felt into the wool without further wool fibres needing to be added. Silk velvets, silk dupion, heavier cottons, metallics and synthetics will almost always need to be anchored into the felt with the addition of a few wisps of wool laid over the top. Wet out again, paying particular attention to the thicker fabrics. Cover with thin plastic and press down to embed the fabrics. Make your sample felt, keeping the plastic covering on until the final stages.

Below: a selection of silk chiffon, organza, habotai and printed rayon, which are all suitable for felting into wool.

While the very fine fabrics like chiffon will become almost part of the felt, the heavier ones will be trapped by the wool and will make a lovely ruched texture when the wool has been fully shrunk.

Applying designs with pre-felts

You can always make pattern on your felt by adding dry fibres during the beginning stages. However, if you would like a more precise and sharper pattern then you can appliqué shapes cut from pre-felt. The pre-felt is the stage when the wool fibres have been wet out, rubbed for a while and the fibres have begun to entangle. The wool can be picked up without falling apart, but it has not yet begun to shrink. This is important because the fibres must still be able to tangle with the base felt and become attached.

You may cut your pattern from the wet pre-felt or you can allow it to dry first. You could use a paper template to cut precise shapes, or cut them freehand. If these shapes are placed on to dry fibres then they will merge more into the background felt than if they are applied to already wet and flattened fibres. After covering with thin plastic, pressure should be applied to the appliqué pattern, before continuing to finish the felt in the usual way.

Above: the motifs on this jacket were created by applying pre-felt shapes to a pre-felt base.

Making an embellished pill-box hat

This little hat looks equally good on a man, woman or a child. It is easy to make and, because it is made flat, can be constructed by a relatively inexperienced feltmaker, before three-dimensional techniques have been mastered. It could be made just using wool fibres for the patterning, or embellished with fabrics. For something more special and elaborate, free-machine embroidery or hand embroidery could be added, maybe using silk or wool threads. Flowers made as described in the section on making corsages (see pages 32–33) could also be stitched or pinned on.

Below: the felt for this little hat was embellished with fabrics and embroidered before being stitched into a hat.

1 Lay out wool tops approximately 75 x 20cm (30 x 8in) deep to make the band. Make two to three fine, even layers at right angles to each other. Arrange another two to three layers in an oval shape 30 x 25cm (12 x 10in), for the crown. Embellish with fabrics or a pattern of wool and silk fibres in the lower half of the strip (see figure 1) and all over the crown oval (see figure 2).

Figure 1: embellish the hat band.

Figure 2: embellish the top of the hat.

2 Make the felt in the usual way, rinse and dry. Embroider by hand or with a sewing machine, if you wish.

3 Put the oval piece on to the crown of a hat block and steam with an iron to make a close-fitting shape (see figure 3). Pin the back edges of the band together to fit the block. Pin the strip to the crown around the block with the pattern side hidden. If you do not possess a hat block you could use a pan or a bowl that has the same circumference as the head to be fitted.

Figure 3: place the oval piece on to the hat block and steam.

Figure 4: attach the band to the crown.

4 Try the hat on and adjust the fitting. When satisfied with the fit, stitch the back seam of the band and attach it to the crown, using small, hidden stitches (see figure 4). Fold back the embellished band to reveal the finished hat.

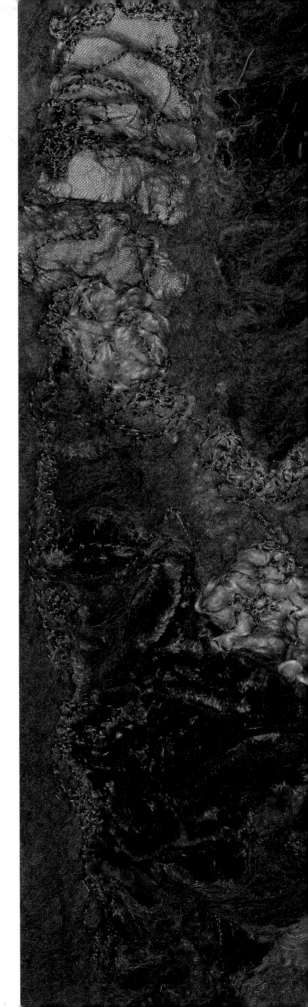

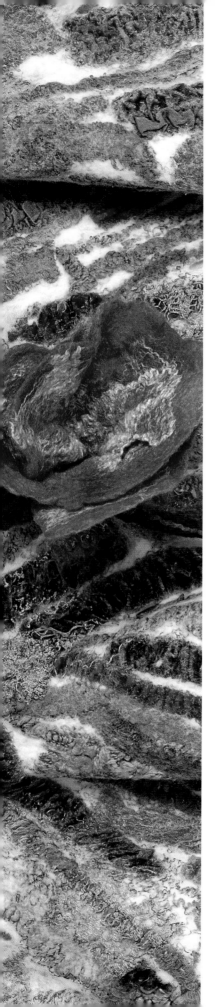

Making a felted embroidered collar

This sumptuous collar is made using two layers of water-soluble plastic with wool fibres and fabrics placed between the layers.

Draw a semi-circle and two quarter circles, with a radius of 45cm (18in), on to rectangles of the soluble plastic. Cut a neck shape 7.5cm (3in) across from the centre on each piece. Lay wool fibres radiating out from the neck edge, on top of the plastic.

Make a selection of fabrics including silks and velvets. Choose some yarns and silk fibres and if you can find some, a little gold fabric or ribbon, to give an opulent look. Arrange the yarns, fabrics and fibres radiating out from the neck edge on top of the wool. Place another layer of the soluble plastic on top, sandwiching the fibres.

Place this in an embroidery hoop and free-machine embroider over the work with embroidery threads. It will have to be stitched in sections, moving the hoop around after finishing each part. Make sure that each fabric is completely stitched around the edges, as there will be no wool fibres trapping them in.

Dissolve the plastic in water. The collar will still be quite fragile at this stage as no felting has taken place. Use hot soapy water to make the felt, shrinking it well to get maximum texture from all the fabrics. Pull into shape before drying flat. If you wish to cover the reverse of the collar to hide the stitching then use a fine silk to hand stitch a lining.

The collar can be fastened with a decorative button and loop, or make a tie from one of the fabrics you have used, to fasten in a bow at the neck. It may also be worn around the waist as a peplum. This collar is finished with a felt corsage (see page 32).

Above: this circular collar is made by layering wool fibres, fabrics and yarns between layers of water-soluble plastic and machine embroidery.

Making hats

Felt beret

Berets never really go out of fashion and at times are very fashionable. Because of the simplicity of the shape there is plenty of opportunity to add embellishment, be it embroidery, beads or a brooch. The edges of the beret could also be shaped, by cutting the template with an undulating edge or maybe making it square, triangular or star-shaped, as shown below. The stalk does not have to be in the centre. Several small ones could be embedded all over the top when laying out the fleece. Maybe add some strips of fabric. Have fun designing your hat.

For a traditionally shaped beret, make a circular template using plastic foam underlay. For a small- to average-size beret, cut the circle with a diameter of 30–35cm (12–14in). If you would like a larger, more flamboyant one then make it with a diameter of 40cm (16in).

Make a stalk first by following the instructions for making a spike or cord (see page 29). Leave a dry root at one end. The stalk can be any length you like or could even be a cluster of thin strings.

Following the instructions for making a blocked hat (see page 61), make the beret using three fine, even layers on each side of the resist, folding the wool in carefully round the edges using the thin plastic and avoiding too much bulkiness. When you have finished laying out the wool, attach the stalk, rooting it in well with extra fibres (see figure 1). Work the edges of the template well before rolling the beret in all directions.

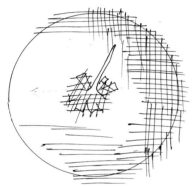

Figure 1: build up three fine layers of wool over the template and attach the stalk (see page 29).

Right: Evelyn Refsahl's exuberant starfish hat could be made using the beret method by shaping the template edges.

When the template has begun to distort inside your hat, choose which side is to be the underside of your beret. Make a circular template 12cm (5in) in diameter. Place it in the centre of the underside and cut a hole for your head. Squeeze out some of the water and try the beret on for size, stretching this hole to fit. Using soapy hands, felt the edges of the hole. Continue to shrink the beret by immersing it in hot water and rolling in soapy hands until it is firm. Rinse and pull it into shape before leaving it to dry. If you would like a sharp edge to your beret, give it a press while it is damp.

Seamless blocked hats

The process of making blocked hats is one of my favourites. They are relatively quick to make and can incorporate many different techniques, especially as I like hats to be slightly flamboyant. Although they are made flat on a template, with sufficient added fullness and maybe a flap or two, the final blocking stages can be very sculptural (see pages 60–61). Small strips of velvet or silk can be added to give a rich and luxurious appearance. Cords or spikes may be rooted in and tied together or beaded. The possibilities are as extensive as your imagination.

Below: there are three flaps on this hat, which have been incorporated during the laying out stage. Holes have been cut in the flaps before the final felting (see page 43 for more information on flaps).

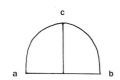

Figure 1.

Making a template for a felt hat

1 Measure around the head, from the top of the forehead and just below the widest part of the bulge at the back. An average head measurement would be 56–57cm (22–22½in) for a woman and slightly larger 58cm (23in) for a man. A difference of only 1cm (½in) either way could be the difference between a large head and a small head. Measure over the top of the head from the same points (see figure 1).

2 Divide the head circumference measurement in two and on paper draw a straight horizontal line to that measurement, marking the ends A and B. Mark the centre of that line and draw a vertical line equalling half the measurement over the top of the head. Mark the top of this line C. Draw a smooth curve from both ends of the line (A–B) touching the vertical line at C, thus forming the crown of the hat (see figure 2).

3 Add some shaping to the hat. As it stands it will make a head-hugging hat. Add fullness, height and a brim, if you like (see figure 3).

4 Shrinkage will be approximately one third, therefore add an extra 50 per cent to make three equal parts; 50 per cent will be half the measurement between A and B. Divide this measurement in half and add it equally all around the hat shape (see figure 4). Cut this out and transfer it to the material chosen for your template. Ideally plastic foam underlay will be used but, as explained in Using Resists and Templates (see page 40), flexible builders' plastic, bubble-wrap, calico sheeting or cardboard will do.

Figure 2.

Figure 3.

Figure 4.

Right: a variety of shapes may be added to the template to give interesting design details. When blocking points can be folded or pleated in.

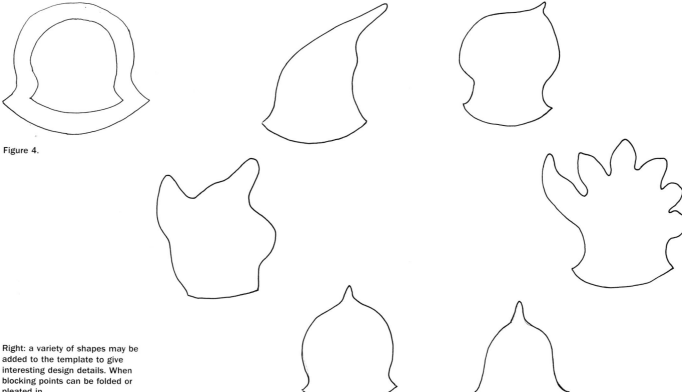

To make a blocked hat using a resist

1 Follow the instructions for using resists to make a seamless item (see page 46). At step 5 keep rolling and stretching the hat until the template cannot be pulled flat inside the hat. Continue with step 6. The hat needs to be shrunk to the required size, i.e. to fit the head of the wearer.

2 Select the required block and stretch the hat over it, securing it at the bottom with some wide elastic. Pull and stretch the top to make a smooth fit, soaping or ironing with a damp cloth to ease and shrink away any wrinkles. Add design details such as pleating, tucking, folding, brims and so on.

3 When you are satisfied with the style and shape, remove the hat from the block and rinse in cold water to remove all traces of soap. Roll the hat in a towel to remove the excess water, and re-shape it on the hat block. Leave it to dry. Please note that the felt will actually dry quicker if removed from the block and stuffed with plastic bags to keep its shape.

4 Any pleats can be ironed a little when dry to make them more permanent. If necessary, a few small, invisible stitches may be added on the inside to hold any pleats in place. Brims may also be pressed to flatten or shape when dry, using a damp cloth.

Below: this hat was made with a pointy template (shown above) and embellished with inlaid velvets and silk fibres.

**Seamless felt
jacket**

When making felt to wear, it is very important that the wool is shrunk to be as firm and tight as possible to avoid excess pilling or bobbling. At the same time it needs to remain fine and flexible. If the wool is initially laid out too thickly, then when fully felted it will become very stiff and it will be difficult for the wearer to move his or her arms. Hopefully by the time you are ready to attempt a jacket you will have experimented widely and will be able to lay the fleece in a fine and even way. You will have a good idea how much to allow for shrinkage when making your template. You may have made a beautifully fine and even three-dimensional sample using only two layers of wool. Now you will be ready to make a jacket.

Making the template or pattern

People often tell me that they would be unable to make a jacket because their pattern-cutting skills are not good enough. Cutting patterns for felt is so different from making patterns for dressmaking that I don't think this is relevant. Feltmaking patterns do not need to be so precise, as felting is not a precise science and there can be so many variables. Much of the fitting can be done by moulding and working on areas of fullness to make them fit. This is why I have stressed the importance of sampling first so that you can estimate how much your own specific felt shrinks when laid out and worked by you. As a starting point, I work on a shrinking factor of about one third, which means the pattern must be made 50 per cent bigger in each direction. For example, for a finished size of 15 x 15cm (6 x 6in) you would need a template of 22.5 x 22.5cm (9 x 9in). I always use the plastic foam that is used for laminate flooring underlay and available from DIY shops.

Measurements needed

- Around the bust
- Waist
- Hips, if the jacket is to cover them
- Nape of the neck to the waist
- Arm length from the neck to the wrist
- Across the back from the middle of the armhole
- Around the top of the arm

Opposite: the finished jacket should be soft, so keep the layers fine.

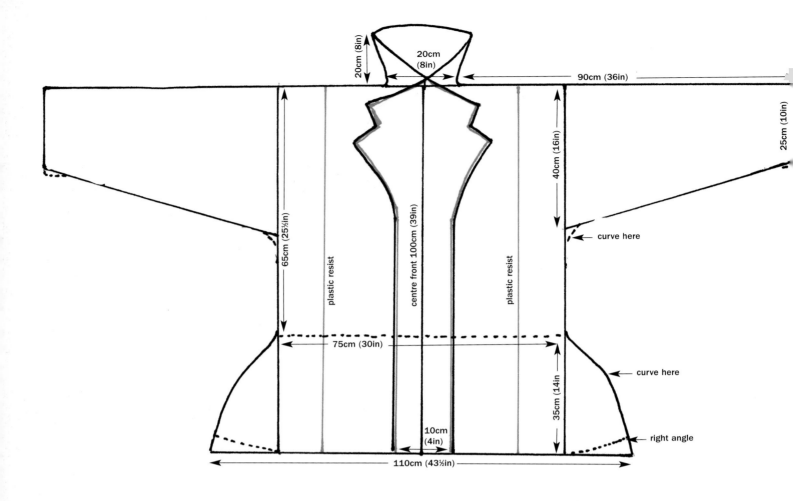

Diagram labels:

20cm (8in)

20cm (8in)

90cm (36in)

25cm (10in)

40cm (16in)

65cm (25½in)

plastic resist

centre front 100cm (39in)

plastic resist

curve here

curve here

right angle

75cm (30in)

35cm (14in)

10cm (4in)

110cm (43½in)

Making a template

Draw the template on paper first, following the instructions given here. The pattern shown is for a finished bust size of 95–100cm (37–39in) and a finished length of 65cm (25½in). It will not be difficult to lengthen or shorten the pattern to your own requirements using the measurements taken on the previous page. The measurements are calculated with a shrinkage factor of one third. Use the diagram to help follow the instructions.

1 Draw a rectangle 100cm (39in) long x 75cm (30in) wide. Draw a line for the centre front. Draw a horizontal line for the waist 65cm (25½in) down.
2 At the top, make a funnel shape with a width at the neck edge of 20cm (8in) and approximately 20cm (8in) high. From the top of the collar continue a line down, making a collar rever. Repeat this for each side of the front, continuing down to make a front extension, or wrap, of 10cm (4in).
3 Make the sleeves 90cm (36in) long, measuring from the neck edge. The sleeve depth is 40cm (16in) narrowing to 25cm (10in) at the wrist. Curve the underarm line, as shown.
4 At the bottom edge extend 17.5cm (7in) from each side to make a total width of 110cm (43½in). Draw curved lines up to the waist for the hip shaping.
5 Transfer the pattern to the template material and draw in the front extension and rever markings.
6 Cut a length of thin plastic approximately 50 x 100cm (20 x 39in) and place it over the markings on the template and trace them through.

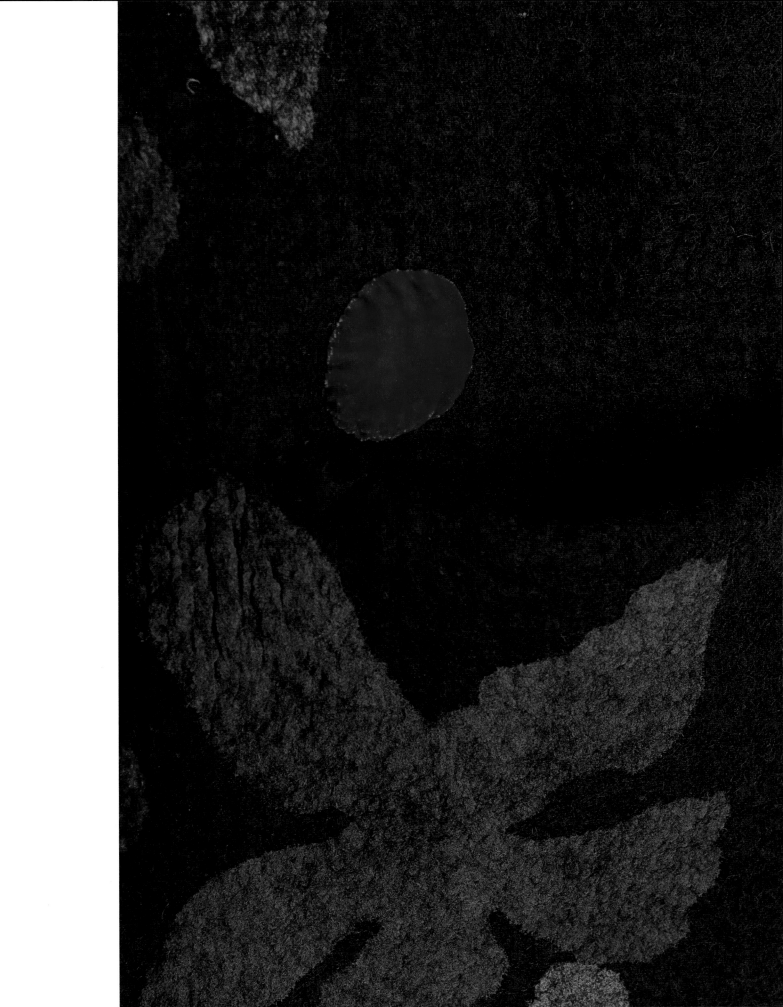

Method

Choose a space big enough to accommodate your template. If a large surface is unavailable, lay out half the garment, roll it up in the thin plastic and lay out the other half.

1 Cover the work surface with a piece of bubble-wrap that is bigger than the template, bubbles facing upwards. Cover that with thin plastic to enable the project to be turned over without the fibres moving. Place your template on top with the back facing up, and lay out your wool tops, keeping the fibres in one direction, and overlapping the edges of the template by about 2.5cm (1in). Make sure that there are no gaps in the fleece. Make a second layer of wool at right angles to the first. Add any pattern or embellishment.

2 Sprinkle warm, soapy water over the surface of the wool. This always takes more water than you expect. Avoid touching the fleece with your hands, as this is likely to displace it. Add any surface decoration either at this stage, or after the wool has been flattened. Cover it with thin plastic and spread the water by pressing gently and removing the air. It helps to sprinkle water on to the plastic to enable your hands to move freely over the surface. When the wool is thoroughly wet and flat, using a roller, carefully roll the jacket inside the two layers of plastic and turn the whole bundle over.

3 Working slowly around the template, fold the layers over the edges, ensuring that you do not build up too much thickness at the corners. Enclose the hem and the bottom of the sleeves completely. (Note: if your two layers are different colours the edges will have to be folded in one at a time and filled in with the matching colour.) Lay a strip of wool along the lines of the first front wrap, fill in this section and wet out.

Above: the velvet spots and motifs are stitched onto the jacket when it is finished. A few wool fibres are placed under the velvet to give a slightly raised surface.

4 Place the thin plastic resist with the wrap marking drawn on it, over the centre, matching up the front edge. Press down to spread the water. Lay wool in the same way over the opposite side up to the front wrap edge. Wet out with soapy water and cover this side with thin plastic, pressing down well again to remove the air and ensure the wool is thoroughly wet. Wet the surface of the plastic.

5 Start felting by gently massaging the edges of the garment, working inwards so that the wool does not spread out from the edges and form ridges. Turn the jacket over using the roller and massage this side.

6 Fold the arms in over the body of the jacket, still wrapped in the thin plastic. Using the roller, roll the garment up tightly, gently squeezing out any excess water that may be oozing out. Wrap a towel round the bundle and tie the roll tightly. Roll about 100 times, unwrap, make a quarter turn and re-roll. Repeat the rolling until the felt has been rolled in each direction. Remove the plastic covering from the surface and inspect the felt. Apply the pinch test to make sure that the fibres have felted together. If it looks a little dry apply more hot, soapy water. Replace the thin plastic on the surface of the jacket, gently roll up without the roller and squeeze the bundle, manipulating the felt. If the template has begun to curl up because the garment is shrinking, remove the plastic sheeting and start cutting the bottom of the sleeves and the hem open. Try to avoid cutting the template. Do not remove the template at this stage.

7 The cut edges will now need to be sealed or felted. Using soapy hands, gently rub the rough edges against the bubble-wrap. Roll the jacket up in the bubble-wrap again and continue rolling until there has been more shrinking and the felt is becoming thicker and stronger. You may now treat the felt a little more vigorously. Keeping it wet and soapy, roll and gently drop on to the table. Continue until the felt has become firm and is the size that you require.

8 Finally, rinse the jacket in cold water to remove all the soap. If you have a spin dryer (not a tumble dryer) this is great for removing the excess water, so that you can try it on for size. Stretch the jacket into shape and dry it flat. You may press the jacket with an iron on a wool setting, for a smooth finish.

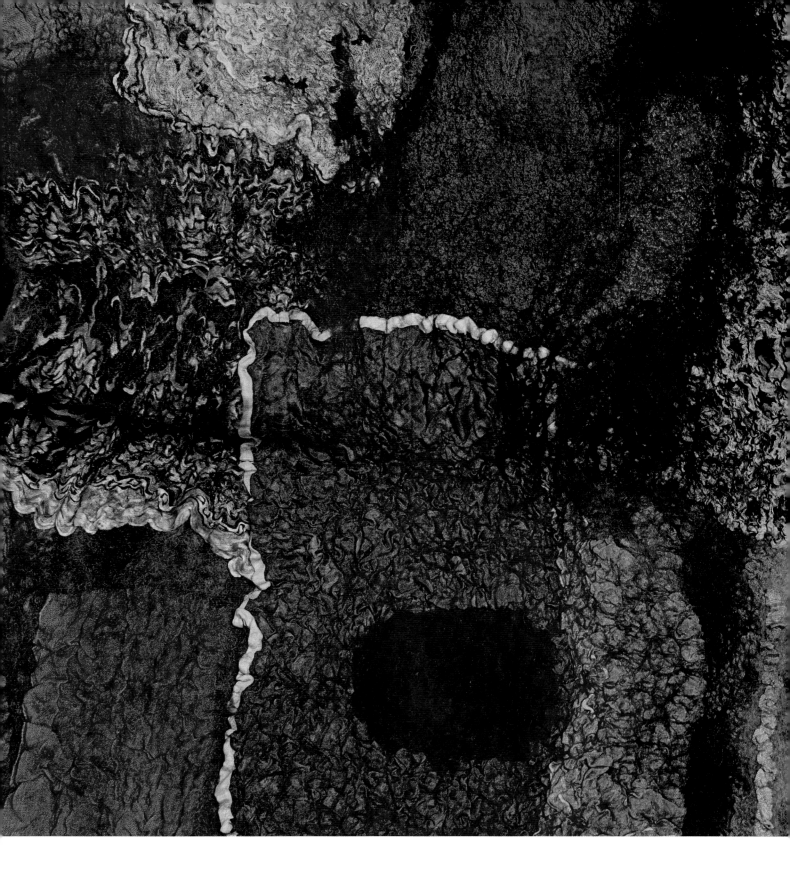

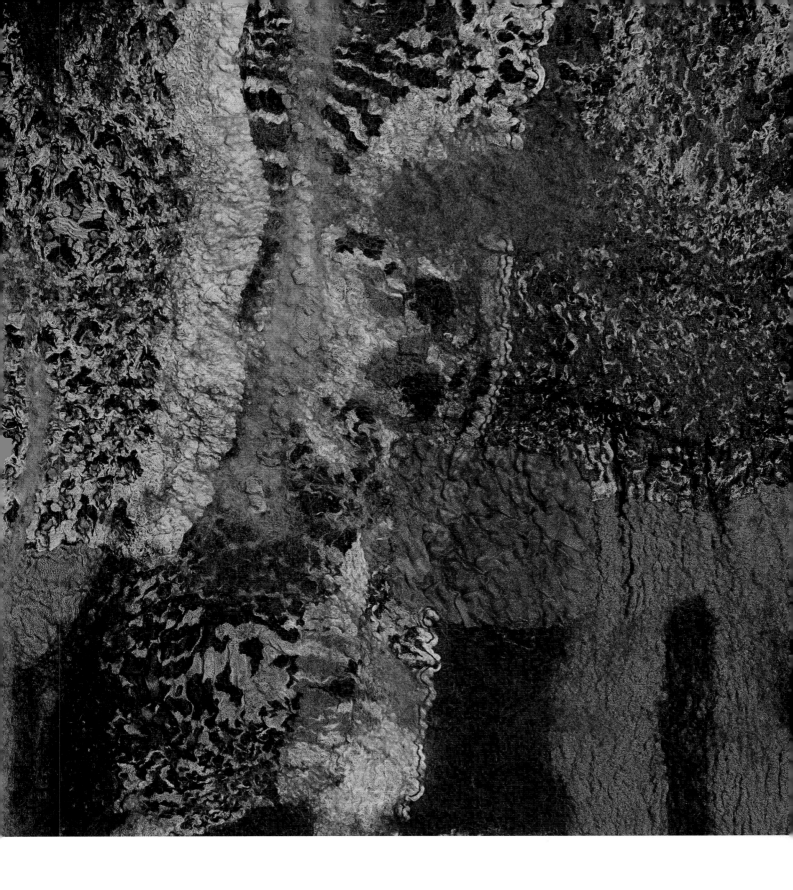

Nuno felt

Until I saw my first piece of nuno felt I had no idea that felt could be so fine and delicate, and drape so well. With a background in fashion, thick rough felt did not hold any great fascination for me, although it was intriguing to watch the felting process and the textile evolving. This nuno technique was something I had to learn!

Unlike traditional felt, thousands of years old, nuno felt was only devised about 15 years ago. Polly Stirling, a feltmaker living in Australia, strived to make a fabric more suitable for the climate there. Together with Sachiko Kotaka, her Japanese friend who regularly worked with her, they experimented widely, incorporating different fabrics, and found that in combination with fine fabric, a minimum amount of wool needed to be used. She and Sachiko coined the name nuno felt, *nuno* being the Japanese word for cloth.

In making felt using this technique, which is also sometimes known as laminated felt, the wool fibres are actually worked through the fabric before the felting and shrinking process is started. The fabrics most suitable to use include chiffon or georgette in silk or viscose, silk habotai, cotton voile, muslin, cheesecloth or fabrics with a slightly loose or open weave. Natural fabrics are best and easiest to use, but with perseverance some synthetics can also work and can give stunning effects. Do experiment with synthetics when you have mastered the technique. Choose a suitable fabric by blowing through it and if you can feel your breath it is likely to work. The most wonderful thing about nuno, apart from its draping qualities and its lightness, is the amazing textures that can be achieved. If the base fabric is only partly covered with wool, when felted and the wool shrinks, the fabric doesn't shrink, but is pulled by the wool and becomes crinkled. The spaces left when laying out the wool can be random, or they can be arranged in a specific pattern. The resulting felt may be reversible.

Left: nuno-felt scarf of silk chiffon, showing flower motifs applied finely with wool.

Opposite: hand-dyed nuno-felt scarf with silk and wool fibres worked in stripes.

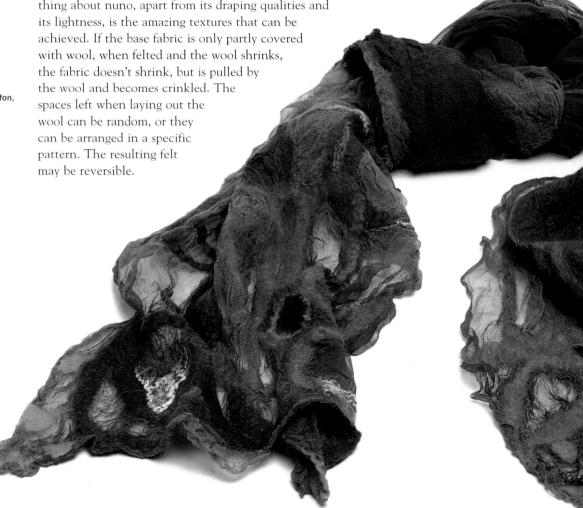

How it works

Unlike traditional felt, where two or more layers of wool are used, it is possible – and usual – to use only one layer. When the little scales on the wool fibres open up when wet, they need to be worked through the weave of the fabric and then to hook around the woven fibres. It sounds more complicated than it is, but just remember that hot water should not be used in the initial stages as it is important that no shrinkage should take place until the wool has been worked through the fabric.

Because synthetic fibres are so slippery, it is difficult for the wool fibres to hook on to them. It is, therefore, sometimes necessary to spread a few fine wisps of wool over the reverse of the fabric for the wool to hook on to once the migration has taken place. The shrinkage of nuno felt is greater than that of traditional felt. I usually work on a shrinkage factor of 50 per cent and therefore make the base fabric twice as big, in each direction, as I wish the finished size to be. You will have to make your own samples to establish your own shrinkage and how much fabric to use.

Getting started

Using a selection of fabrics from those described on page 72, cut 30cm (12in) squares. Pull out fine amounts of fibres from your wool tops and lay them on the fabric. There needs to be only one layer of wool for this method. Cover some of the fabrics all over with fibres and others with patterns or grids so that you can see the different effects possible when shrunk. The wool will shrink most along the length of the fibres.

1 Sprinkle cool soapy water over the fibres and, using thin plastic sheeting over the top, press down the wool until it is flat. Remember that using hot water would cause the wool to felt before the fibres have worked through the fabric so they won't attach to it. Wet the top plastic so that your hands will easily slide over it, rub the surface to get rid of the air and spread the water, ensuring the fibres are thoroughly wet. Supporting the fabric on the plastic, flip it over to the fabric side. You will be able to see any dryness remaining and wet it, if necessary.

2 Roll the felt in bubble-wrap in the usual felting way, keeping the plastic sheeting on the wool side. The wool fibres will begin to work through the fabric. When you can see them and the fabric is beginning to crinkle a little, add some soap to your hands and scrunch the felt, dropping it gently several times on to the table.

3 Complete the shrinking and felting by rubbing the fabric side on the bubble-wrap. Dip the felt in hot water, squeeze out, keep it soapy and continue until it will shrink no more. Do not stop shrinking too soon. For anything wearable it is important that the felt is shrunk as much as possible, which could be 50 per cent or more, to prevent it pilling or becoming fluffy.

4 Rinse your samples in cold water and stretch them back into shape. Measure them and calculate the shrinkage.

Opposite: samples of nuno felt on chiffon and habotai silk, showing the different effects that can be achieved when the wool tops are placed in different ways – grids, stripes and random patterns.

Using fabric for strength

It is possible to use fabric and lay wool on both sides to create a light but strong fabric. The wool should be laid very finely in order to maintain the draping qualities of the fabric. Alternatively, the wool may be sandwiched between two layers of fabric. The result will be a soft quilted effect. The wool should be laid slightly thicker using this method, for most effective results.

Cutting fabrics for nuno-felt garments

Most of the patterns I use for nuno felt are cut as a square or rectangle, except the sleeves, which need a bit of shaping. Chiffon is notoriously difficult to cut in a straight line and must be pinned very carefully. Although this is never recommended for dressmaking, as fabric that is not woven entirely straight can affect the hang of a garment, wherever possible I do think it is easier to tear the fabrics. In nuno felting any unevenness in the base fabric will disappear with the shrinking. Also the resulting frayed edges do attach very well to the felt. Do test a small piece carefully first though, as some fabrics are just too fine and can end up with rather a lot of pulled threads, and will have to be cut. Put a small snip through the selvedge and tear across to test.

Sleeves are often cut the full width of the fabric, so tear two lengths equalling the sleeve length. Fold each in half, lengthwise and place one on top of the other. Pin the edges together, all round. Draw the sleeve shape on to the top fabric and cut through all four layers at once.

It is often easier to remove the selvedges of the fabric as they are sometimes too densely woven for the wool to felt through. However, I don't usually remove them when making scarves as they can contribute to making a very interesting and decorative edge, especially when caught in with the wool.

The other important factor to bear in mind, especially if you do not have very much fabric, is that the straight grain is unimportant: you can use the fabric in any direction. Because you are making a completely new fabric and the base fabric will be fully ruched up with the shrinking, the starting direction is irrelevant.

Finishing the edges of nuno felt

Finishing the edges of nuno felt is rather different from those of traditional felt. The fabric used will dictate how it is going to look. I personally favour a rather organic finish and am often happy to leave it, however it turns out. Sometimes the edges are caught in with the wool and are pulled, and where the wool has not been placed right up to the edge then a little frill may form. Occasionally, however, these edges do not look good and need to be pulled out and unfolded. I often exaggerate the organic nature by cutting away some of the fabric bits and making a feature of an undulating hemline, or even cutting away fabric to make holes. If wool surrounds the hole it will heal well. If I was going to cut it anyway, then I would do this before the final shrinking so that the wool will felt.

However, it is possible to have a straight hem, if that is what you prefer, by using the thin plastic to fold the edges from the beginning or enclosing them with wool.

Fabric-collaged nuno felt

Beautiful effects can be made in nuno felt just by spreading the fleece thinly over the surface of the woven base fabric or by leaving parts of the fabric uncovered. When the wool shrinks and felts, the fabric is pulled, forming crinkles or ruching, depending on the fabric's qualities. It is possible though, as it is in traditional felting, to add a variety of other materials to give a rich and sumptuous surface.

Below: sample of nuno felt embedding a variety of different silk fabrics, fibres and net.

Fine silk, for example like habotai, will blend very easily and form a scrunchy texture, whereas silk or rayon chiffon can become so embedded as to become almost indistinguishable from the felt. Heavier silk fabric like dupion will need to be trapped or 'glued' into place with fleece underneath, and a few fibres also over the top, but will give very exciting textures. Try using a variety of different fabrics from velvets, metallics and fine cottons to rayons and prints. Think about using recycled clothing and scarves. Experiment to see which fabrics will anchor themselves in and which will need to be 'glued' in. Make yourself a sampler with as many different materials as you can find.

Fabrics that don't have an open enough weave to be trapped by the wool fibres can be appliquéd using a few stitches or embroidery, which in turn can add an extra dimension to the overall texture of your work.

Further texture may be incorporated into your nuno felt by adding shapes cut from felt that has already been fully felted. The shapes may be sandwiched between the wool and the fabric at the laying out stage and felted in. The finer the base fabric is, the more defined the shapes will be.

Below: close-up detail of a jacket with hand-dyed silk on the surface, showing how the different weights of silk react with the shrinking.

Using recycled fabrics

I find it very hard to get rid of clothing when the fabric is a beautiful colour or an exciting print. Obviously not all the fabrics will be suitable to use for felting, but most textile artists will have ideas for using those that are not. Many of my designer and artist friends are currently chopping up all kinds of old garments into strips and making rag rugs or shopping bags. Fashion bags are made using, perhaps, the pockets and design details of previously worn garments and clothing is refashioned into catwalk creations. If you visit charity shops you will usually find a collection of silk or viscose chiffon scarves. Try to imagine what the design on the material will look like when it has become nuno felt. The print will ruche and gather. Even the dullest and most unexciting patterns, with the addition of wool fibres and some texture, can become most alluring.

This stole was made using a selection of what I thought were some of my most boring scraps of fabric, together with some more interesting ones. The silk sari that I have incorporated here was particularly useful as there were three or four different aspects of the design and also of the weave, from fine chiffon areas to heavier sateen sections. It was an exciting challenge to make everything work together and with the addition of a few silk fibres too, it was gradually built up section by section, without any stitching. Although wool was used to join all the pieces, in many places extra wool was added either on the reverse or on the surface to encourage more texture. It was finally shrunk once all the fabrics were firmly attached together. All the pieces could also have been stitched in a patchwork before laying out the wool fibres. This would have given a different effect.

Heavier fabric, which may not have an open enough weave for the wool fibres to migrate through, may need to be stitched into place, or to be appliquéd. If this is done before the shrinking and wool fibres are placed beneath the fabric then the stitches will be a further addition to the texture.

Suitable seams for joining nuno felt

It is not always necessary to stitch the fabric of nuno felt as it is often possible to felt the seams together. As long as there is wool between the layers of fabric the fibres can be worked through both layers and be quite strong. However, to stop the fabric slipping apart during the felting process it is sometimes advisable to put a stitch in, even if it is a tacking stitch that can be removed later. If the stitches show, they will be easy to remove, but if they don't, it won't matter. This method would be used when working a garment over a template.

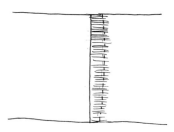

Joining fabrics without stitching.

Large garments are often easier to make flat and then joined together before the final shrinking process. After the pre-felt stage the separate garment pieces can be dried, as it is easier to stitch dry fabrics. The method you choose to use will depend on the thickness of your base fabric.

If you wish to use a sewing machine, set the machine width to about a 1.5 zig-zag stitch with a length of about 2. Trim away the excess wool that has extended beyond the edges, so that you are stitching the actual fabric. With the fabric sides of the garment together, stitch the seams very close to the edges, or over them. Trim close to the stitching and press flat so that when the seam is covered by extra wool it will not become too bulky. The seam will be on the wool side of the fabric.

Zig-zag seam.

Alternatively, use a straight stitch with a tiny seam, which you can trim close to the stitching or open out and press flat. This seam, also, should be on the wool side of the fabric. Cover the seams with wool fibres, wet and work well before the final shrinking of your garment. The seams will disappear with the shrinking.

The third method is a lapped seam where the pre-felted pieces are kept flat and one is lapped over the other by about 0.5cm (¼in). It is then stitched down the centre. As long as there is wool to the edges, the seam should almost disappear with the final shrinking.

Opposite: this scarf is made from two different lengths of silk chiffon joined down the centre by overlapping and felting together.

Below: Sachiko Kotaka made this shawl by using well-felted felt as pre-felt. Cotton and wool fabrics were appliquéd on the surface before felting again.

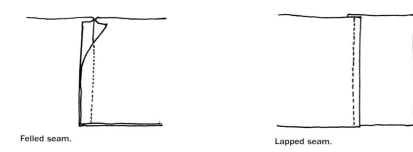

Felled seam.   Lapped seam.

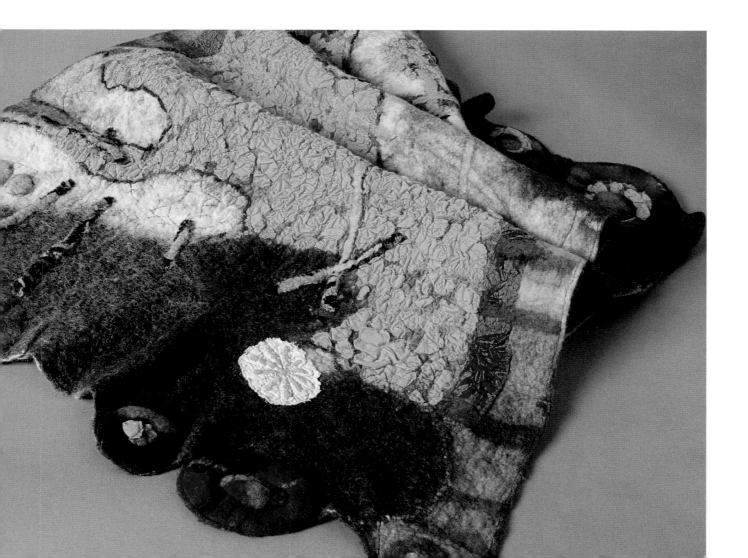

Below: nuno-felt scarf using hand-dyed silk fabric with a hand-dyed silk and wool border. The fibres have been worked on to the body of the scarf following the markings in the silk.

Shawls

With 3m (3¼yd) of fabric you could make a lovely long stole with straight ends. However, without reducing the length, and with careful cutting and joining, a shaped shawl can be made.

Using 90cm (35in) wide fabric, cut triangles from the top corners to a quarter of the way along the bottom edge, as shown in figure 1. Stitch these triangles together along what were the ends of the fabric, i.e. the edges that measure 90cm (35in). This will make another triangle that can be stitched to the shortest edge of the shawl. Keep all the seams on the same side of the fabric.

If you have 3m (3¼yd) of 150cm (60in) wide fabric then a slightly different shape may be made, resulting in a longer length (see figure 2). Cut triangles from halfway down the ends – on this width it will be 75cm (30in), to 75cm (30in) along the bottom. Join each of these to the ends of the shawl. The angles on the bottom edges may be rounded off. As an alternative, they could be stitched to the top edge, making a more curved shape.

Cover with wool fibres and felt in the usual nuno-felt way.

Above: this nuno felt reversible shawl was made using hand-dyed habotai silk and hand-dyed wool fibres.

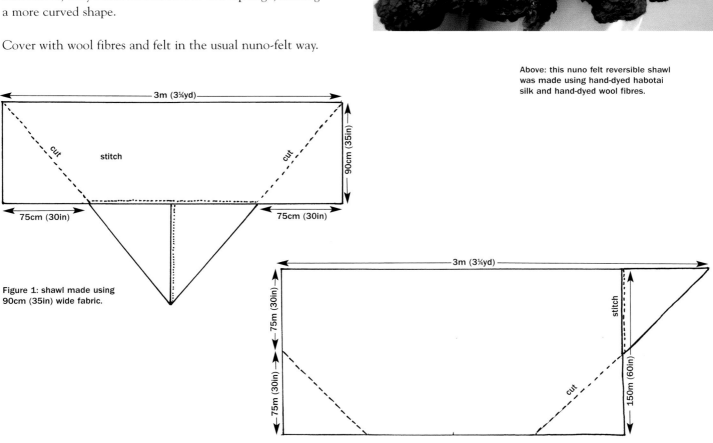

Figure 1: shawl made using 90cm (35in) wide fabric.

Figure 2: shawl made using 150cm (60in) wide fabric.

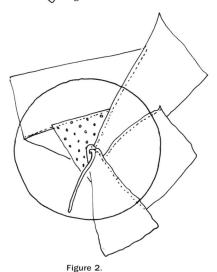

Figure 1.

Figure 2.

Nuno felt berets and blocked hats

Select an assortment of fabrics with natural fibres. These need to be fine enough for the wool to migrate through. Chiffon or georgette in silk or rayon, silk habotai or organza, cotton voile or muslin would all be suitable. If you are able to source some recycled printed scarves, they will add extra interest to your hat. You may also add snippets of velvet, but they will have to be trapped in with wool fibres. The more variations of weights of fabric you choose, the more variation of texture you will get.

Follow the instructions for making the beret or blocked hat (see pages 58–61) to the stage when you have all the layers of wool on the template, and the template is enclosed with wet fibres. Arrange the fabrics over the wool on one side, slightly overlapping the fine ones and cutting heavier ones to shape. Leave enough fabric to bring over to the second side (see figure 1). If you have a stalk, cut a small hole in the fabric and pull it through (see figure 2). When you have finished covering the first side, press the fabric down with thin plastic to make it wet and stick to the wool. You may need to sprinkle on more water at this stage. Cover with the plastic and flip the hat over. Pull the fabrics firmly over the edge of the template to make it smooth. You will have to fit the fabrics to this side by cutting slits and removing pieces, as there will be some fullness when they are pulled over the curve of the edge and you need to reduce excess bulk.

Wet the second side and enclose the hat in plastic sheeting. Continue to felt until the fabrics have bonded to the wool, concentrating at the beginning on the edges to avoid ridges forming. Complete the hat in the usual way. The fabrics will crinkle and ruche as the felt shrinks.

Right: this felt hat is made in the conventional way as described on pages 59–61. The fabrics are arranged once all the wool fibres have been wetted out.

Below: nuno-felt beret with a long stalk. The disc threaded on to the stalk is made from the circle removed for the head fitting.

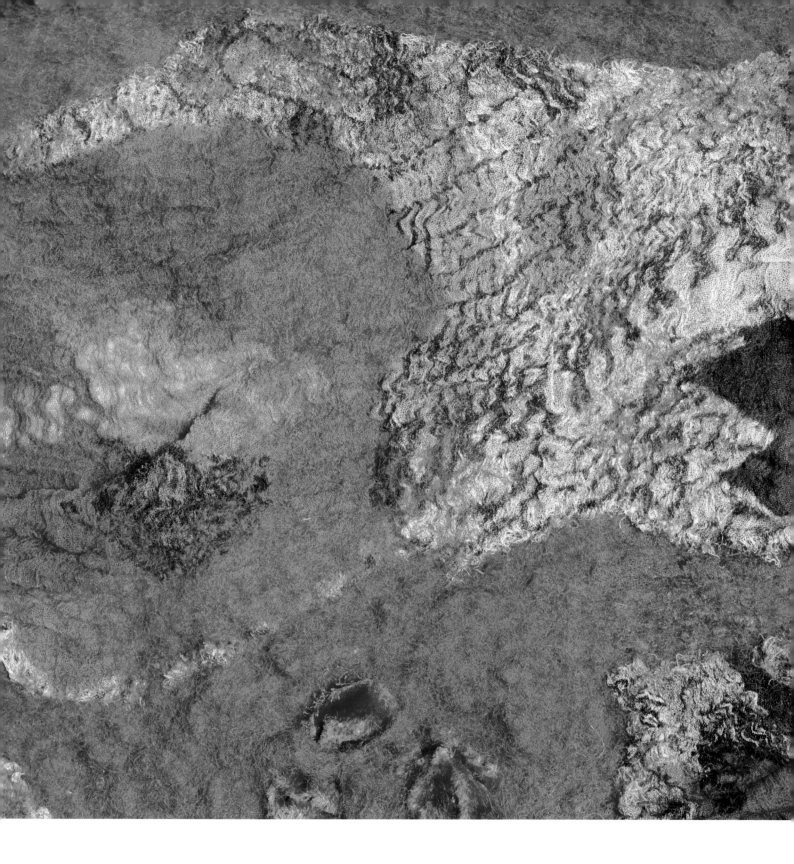

Nuno-felt vest top

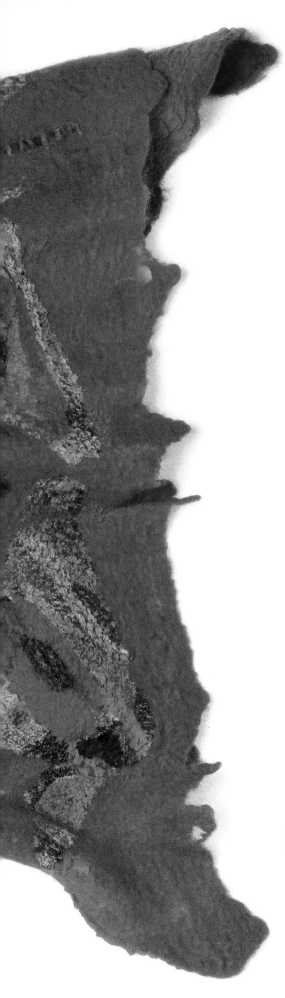

When you have mastered the technique of nuno felt you would probably like to attempt a garment. If you have experimented widely making your nuno felt, you will begin to have some idea how much shrinkage to expect. It is not an exact science as there are many variables. Unless you have accurately calculated the amount required and weighed the wool tops, and you lay them in exactly the same way as your sample, you cannot be entirely sure that it will be the required size when finished. I usually work on a 50 per cent shrinkage rate for my clothing, which means that you will have to start twice as big – in both directions. I maintain that there are always ways and means of further shrinking the finished item, in specific places, when required.

The measurements given are for a basic vest top; however the instructions are for the top that is pictured, which incorporates some recycled vintage fabrics and thin strips of velvet. You may prefer to use one of the other nuno techniques that you have learnt.

This garment is made flat and stitched together at the end. There are ways in which it could be made without visible seams if you prefer (see page 81).

Materials

- 2.2m (2½yd) of 90cm (36in) wide, deep red viscose georgette or silk chiffon
- 100g (3½oz) of deep pink merino wool tops
- Deep red silk/viscose velvet cut into narrow strips
- Flower motifs cut from printed silk or viscose fabric
- Matching sewing machine thread
- A few white silk fibres

Left and opposite: this vest top is made using silk chiffon as a base fabric. Recycled fabrics have been worked into the top layer.

45cm (18in)

220cm (87in)

fold

Figure 1: fold the fabric lengthwise with the selvedges together.

Method

1 Lay your towel on the work surface and place 2.5 x 1m (2¾ x 1yd) of bubble-wrap, bubbles facing upwards, on the towel.

2 Cut the georgette or chiffon as in figures 1 and 2 and remove both selvedges (see page 76 for more information on cutting fabrics). These measurements are for a finished size of 90cm (36in) bust. If a larger size is needed then you can either use a wider fabric or join a strip of fabric down one side before cutting the neck edge. Calculate how much bigger you will need it to be and work out the shrinkage to find the total width required.

3 Spread the fabric on the bubble-wrap, and lay out the wool as shown in figure 3, in all directions, for an even shrinkage. Take care with the neck edge and armholes, that the wool follows the shape and is laid vertically. The hem of this garment is very organic, which I like, but could equally well be made straight and even.

4 Arrange the flower motifs, cut from the fabric, over the wool, and lay the velvet strips in different directions. Trap them into the wool by covering with thin wisps of wool, horizontally along the length. Sprinkle a few wisps of white silk fibres over the garment for added texture and sheen.

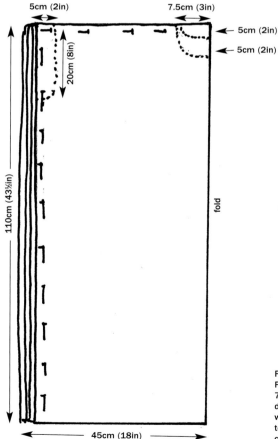

5cm (2in) 7.5cm (3in)

5cm (2in)

5cm (2in)

20cm (8in)

110cm (43½in)

fold

45cm (18in)

Figure 2: fold in half horizontally. From the folded edge, cut away 7.5cm (3in) across by 5cm (2in) down. Cut the armhole away from where the selvedges are pinned together, 5cm (2in) across from the corner and 20cm (8in) down. Unfold the fabric and lower the front neck by another 5–7.5cm (2–3in).

5   Using a cool soap solution in the sprinkler, wet out the vest. Cover the whole piece with thin plastic sheeting and wet the plastic.

6   Rub the surface of the plastic sheeting until the water has spread, all the air has been removed, and the wool is thoroughly wet. You might like to use a screwed-up plastic bag for this process.

7   Using the pipe insulation, tightly roll up the vest in the plastic, but not in the bubble-wrap. Turn the roll over and, with the plastic underneath, carefully unroll so that the chiffon is now on top. You will be able to see if there are any dry spots remaining. Make sure it is wet all over.

8   Re-roll, but this time in the bubble-wrap too. It is important that the bundle is tight. Wrap the towel around the roll to stop any slipping or, if you find it easier, put a tie around each end.

9   Roll 50 times in each direction. The wool should have begun to work through the fabric and a little shrinking will have taken place. The flower motifs will be beginning to crinkle.

10 Remove the vest from the plastic and, using soap solution, work the edges of the garment with your fingers, rubbing against the bubble-wrap.

11 To complete the shrinking, rub the fabric side against the bubbles, keeping it wet at all times. A little warmer water may now be used. Scrunch the garment in your hands and drop it gently on to the table. Repeat all these processes until the vest is the right size. The fabric side can be rubbed against the bubble-wrap. It is possible to shrink specific parts of the garment by rolling tightly on itself, or in the towel. It is necessary to shrink garments fully as they will receive lots of wear.

12 Finally, rinse the vest and squeeze out the excess water with the towel, reshape the vest and leave it to dry.

13 Machine or hand-stitch the side edges together, leaving a slit at the bottom, if you wish.

Figure 3.

Nuno-felt jackets

Above: a printed silk chiffon has been used as the base fabric for this jacket, which makes it reversible. The contours of the spots have been cut during the last stages of shrinking to make a pretty, decorative edge. It follows the same pattern as the bolero (see page 98) except there is a front wrap as shown in figure 3, opposite, and it has a longer sleeve length.

You can choose whether your nuno-felt jacket will have the wool or the fabric on the outside. This decision may affect your choice of base fabric or whether you add any embellishment to the wool side. You may decide to make the jacket reversible, which is perfectly feasible and exciting to do. Some of the jackets I make can also be worn upside down in a short bolero shape with a large shawl collar.

There are two different techniques that I use when making nuno-felt clothing. The one you choose to use may depend on how much space you have available to work on. The first method, making the garment in one piece, is used for the jacket above, and is explained on the following pages (see pages 95–97). The second method, making the garment in sections, is explained on pages 98–99 and used for the bolero on page 99.

Most often I work on flat fabric, cut to size and shape. Most of the jackets I make start with the same way of cutting the fabric (see figures 1 and 2 on pages 90–91). The measurements vary and perhaps the shape of sleeve. I may add different shaping to the fronts (see figure 3, below, and figure 5, overleaf), collar, sleeves (see figure 4) and body. All these are described, but you may use them in any combination.

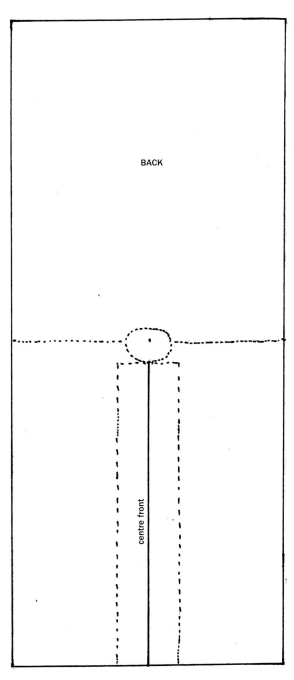

BACK

centre front

Figure 3: add front extensions to create a wrap.

Left: the spots will crinkle and distort as the felt is shrunk.

Right: for a shaped front extension, one option is to use the pieces left over from cutting the sleeves for front extensions on each side. They can be attached by either the diagonal lengths (see figure 5a) or by the straight (see figure 5b). Each way will give a different look and hang.

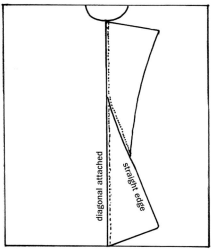

Figure 5a

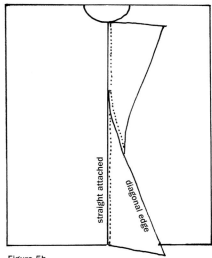

Figure 5b

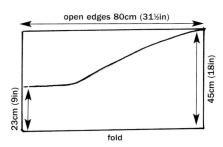

Figure 4a: cut like this for a long cuff.

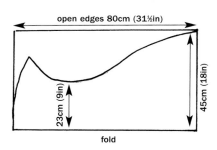

Figure 4b: cut like this for a bell-bottom sleeve.

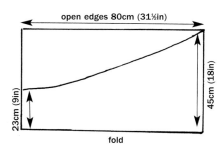

Figure 4c: cut like this for a sleeve with a narrow wrist.

Lay the wool fibres on the fabric, add any decoration and wet with cool, soapy water. Cover with thin plastic and pre-felt each section of the garment by rubbing, then rolling. The fibres should have just started coming through the fabric. Dry the fabric pieces and stitch them together, with the fabric sides together (see figures 6 and 7, opposite). The seams will then appear on the wool side. More wool fibres can be placed over the seams and worked into the felt before proceeding to the next stage.

Plastic is then placed inside the garment and down the sleeves, to stop the back felting to the front, or the sleeves sticking together. Wet the whole garment again with warm water and keep the complete garment enclosed in plastic. Roll tightly around a broomstick or foam pipe, and secure with ties at each end and in the middle. This is to prevent the bundle slipping while you are rolling it. Roll about 50 times. Unroll and check that the jacket is beginning to shrink. Turn the garment 90 degrees and re-roll. Repeat this process until it has been rolled in each direction.

Unroll and remove the jacket from the plastic. Check that the seams and edges have a nice finish to them, and that the edges have not folded over. Immerse the jacket in a bowl of hot water and, adding soap, squeeze and gently drop it on to the bubble-wrap surface several times. Rub the fabric side against the bubble-wrap or on to a washboard, if you have one.

Squeeze out the excess water and try the jacket on for size. It is important that garments are shrunk as much as possible so that the wool will wear well. When you are satisfied with the size and shape of your jacket, rinse it in cold water, remove excess water, re-shape and leave to dry.

Nuno felt may be pressed if you wish, but be aware that sometimes pressing will squash or flatten the texture.

Above: this jacket was made using the diagrams shown on this page.

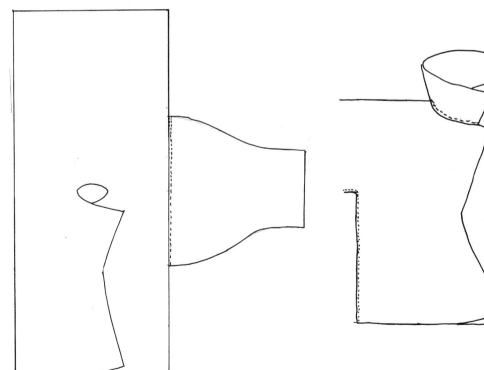

Figure 6: stitch the sleeve to the edge of the jacket, matching the notch markings at shoulder.

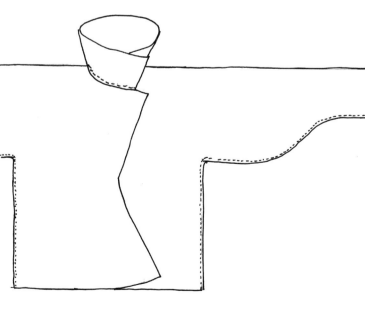

Figure 7: attach the collar to the neck edge. Join the side and underarm seams all in one. Remember to keep all the seams on the wool side.

Nuno-felt bolero

This boxy little jacket is a good one to start with, as there are only three pieces to cut out, or four if you choose to have a shoulder seam. It is an edge-to-edge garment so therefore will not need a front wrap or extension. You will need only 3m (3¼yd) of fabric depending on the size it is to fit. Cut a length of fabric 2m (78in) long and 1m (39in) wide. Fold it in half lengthwise and again in half across the width, matching all the selvedges together, pinning them in place. Mark the shoulders with a tiny snip. Measure from the folded corner 7.5cm (3in) across and 1.5cm (½in) down and cut the neck away (see diagram on pages 90–91).

Unfold and lower the front neck by 2.5cm (1in). From the centre of the front neck cut all the way down to make a front opening. The sleeves are straight all the way down. Cut each sleeve approximately 90–100cm (35–39in) wide and 45cm (18in) long (see diagram below).

Lay wool fibres over all the pieces, add any decoration, wet out and felt to the pre-felt stage. This is the when the wool fibres have begun to migrate through the fabric, but have not yet begun to shrink. Remember to use cool water so that the wool will not felt before it is through the fabric. Leave the pieces to dry and, choosing one of the methods for joining seams (see pages 80–81), match the sleeves to the shoulders and sew across. Join the side seams. Cover the seams with wool fibres and, wetting first, felt the wool. Wet the whole garment and put plastic inside to prevent the sleeves and body felting together. Continue felting until it is fully shrunk.

For a variation, the front edges could be shaped into a curve. Slits could left at the bottom of the side seams or at the sleeve hems.

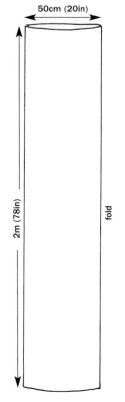

Figure 1: fold the fabric lengthwise with the selvedges together.

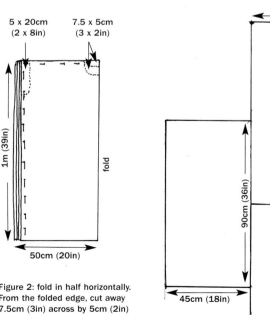

Figure 2: fold in half horizontally. From the folded edge, cut away 7.5cm (3in) across by 5cm (2in) down. Cut the armhole away from where the selvedges are pinned together, 5cm (2in) across from the corner and 20cm (8in) down. Unfold the fabric and lower the front neck by another 5–7.5cm (2–3in).

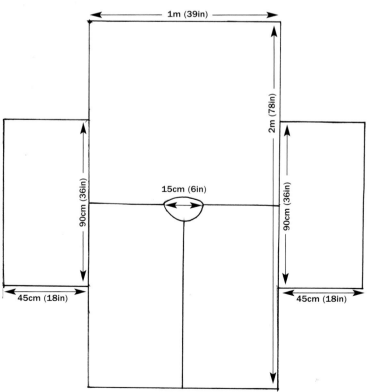

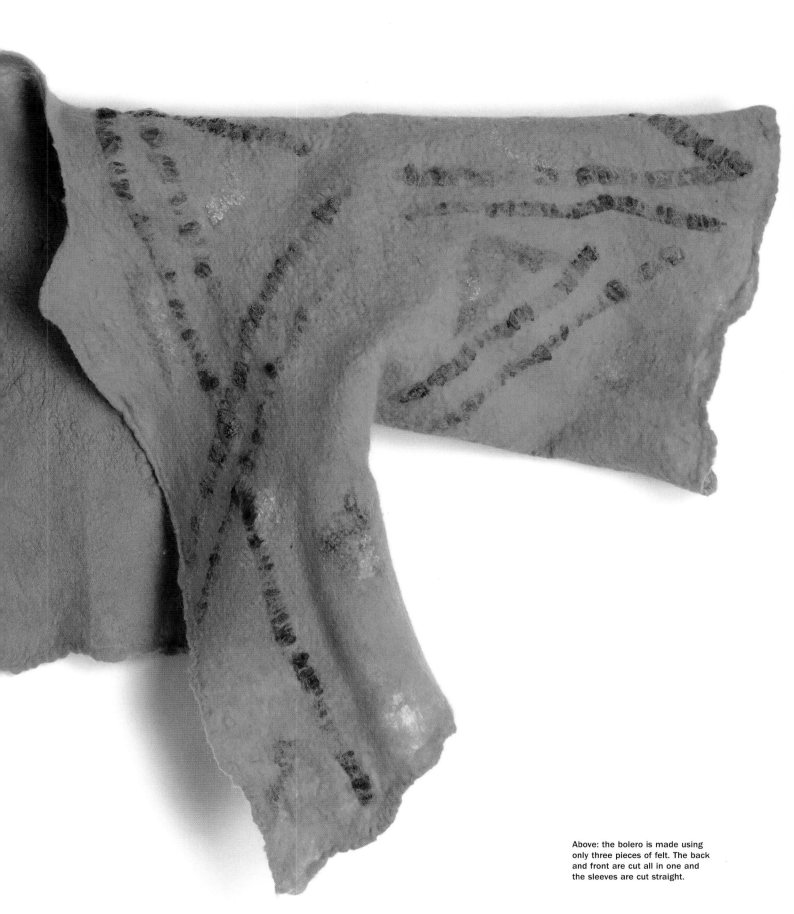

Above: the bolero is made using only three pieces of felt. The back and front are cut all in one and the sleeves are cut straight.

Shaping for jackets

Although it is possible to add shaping to garments by laying the fibres in the direction in which you want them to shrink, there are ways of cutting and shaping the base fabric that you are using that will also help to shape the garment.

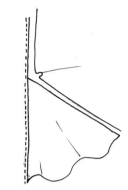

Inserting a godet into a seam.

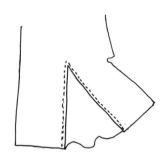

Inserting a godet into a slit.

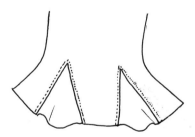

Two godets give extra shaping.

Godets

Godets are used in dressmaking to add fullness and swing to a garment. They are triangles of fabric that are inserted either into a seam or into a slit cut in the fabric. They can be cut any size, ranging from a semi-circle to a small triangle. I often use them when making nuno-felt jackets and coats where I want to have a shaped waist but a wide flared hem. I usually pre-felt the godet before stitching it into the pre-felted garment.

Make the seams on the right side, or whichever is to be the wool side, so that they can be covered over with wool. When stitching a godet into a slit in dressmaking, the pointed end is very difficult to fit neatly. The godet will also appear to be longer than the slit into which it is to be sewn; this is because the slit is on the straight grain of the fabric, and the godet, being a triangle, is slightly on the cross grain, which stretches. Stitch one side of the godet in place at a time. Pin the godet to the slit, matching the top point to the top of the slit and with the hems matching. Ease the remainder to fit, slightly stretching the straight fabric. Any slight puckering or difficulties when using godets with felting, however, will disappear with the shrinking. Felt is very forgiving.

Nuno-felt pockets

These can be made in the same way as normal pockets (see pages 43–45), laying the fabric down first on to the top of the laid-out garment. The fabric will need to extend beyond the resist to felt into the garment and give extra strength. If the pocket is to be only decorative then it will be sufficient to anchor it just with the wool extending on to the garment and the fabric the size of the resist.

Dyeing wool and silk with acid dyes

I love clear, bright and strong colours and have been using commercially dyed fibres, so readily available in about 125 shades, for many years. Colour mixing by blending them together using carders adds another few hundred options, so why go to the palaver of dyeing your own when the colours obtained do not have the same intensity as those achieved with commercial dyes? Well, with a little experimentation, a simple recipe and minimal equipment, very exciting and equally alluring hues can be obtained. The hand-dyed palette tends to be much softer and subtler, but can be dark and rich too. Acid dyes are used for protein fibres such as wool and silk. The acid used in the method described here is vinegar.

When I hand-dye I am looking for a very different effect and do not need an all-over smooth colour. I often put three or four different dyes into the dye-pot at the same time and allow the fibres to absorb the colours separately and also together where they overlap. Fibres and fabrics dyed together result in a co-ordinated range, which may be used together to make nuno-felt garments. While the wool fibres will always have a matt appearance, silk fibres can add a greater brilliance and contrast. Silk fabrics, depending on the weave and quality, will also take the dye in different ways, and will add a variety of textures to your nuno felt.

I have an electric tea urn that I use for dyeing. It is quite narrow so the fabrics are often folded and twisted in the pot and sometimes come out of it with lovely patterns and swirls where some of the dye has not been able to penetrate the fibres. The shibori technique is a more formal way of making these patterns. If there is room in the pot with your fabrics and fibres, add some tied fabrics. Large stainless-steel pans can also be used on a cooker and the technique will be the same. Dye suppliers will usually include instructions for their dyes.

Above: fibres and fabrics can be dyed together for a co-ordinated look. 'French Poppy' coat dress by Mollie Littlejohn is a pieced garment incorporating silk fabric and merino wool.

Above: waistcoat made using layer upon layer of silk chiffons and wool fibres, all dyed separately before construction of the garment.

Method

1 Weigh the fabric and the fibres.
2 Fill the dye bath (usually a stainless-steel pan) with enough water to cover all the fibres easily.
3 Put the wool in to soak until it is completely wet so that it will be able to absorb the dye easily and evenly.
4 Heat the dye pot until hand warm.
5 For every 100g (4oz) of fibres to be dyed, measure 20ml (0.7fl oz) of cold water and add 1 teaspoon of acetic acid (vinegar). Add to the dye pot.
6 For every 100g (4oz) of fibres you will need 2–3g (0.1oz) of dye powder. Dissolve the dye powder in half a cup of hot water, stirring well to get rid of any lumps. Add to the dye pot.
7 We will not be looking for even dyeing using this method, and will use three or four colours at a time. Pour the dyes on to the fibres in sections, overlapping them so that they will mix. Put the fabric on top. Gently push the fabric with a spoon so that it will be submerged. It is very important that the wool is not stirred as, of course, it could become felted in the pot. Cover the pot and bring the heat to 80°C (176°F) or just below boiling point, over a 15-minute period. Simmer for 30–60 minutes. Check the colour of the fibres and remove when you have achieved the results you require. If the water becomes clear then the dye bath will have been exhausted and the fibres will have absorbed all of the dye. To help this along, you may add a teaspoon of citric acid (lemon juice) 15 minutes before the end.
8 Remove the fabric with tongs and rinse until clear. Lift the wool gently into a bowl and allow it to cool before spinning in a spin dryer and drying. Any manipulation of the wet wool before it has had a chance to cool will result in the fibres felting, therefore do not put hot wool into the spinner or into cold water.

Note: pots made of materials other than stainless steel are not usually chosen for dyeing because the methods can affect the colour. Copper can give a greenish cast, for example. Never use the same pot for dyeing and cooking because most dyes are toxic.

Right: detail showing silks that have been dyed using a shibori technique of tying the fabric around a pole with string and scrunching before placing in the dye pot. The string will resist the dye and very interesting effects can be achieved.

Nuno-felt jacket
using a template

Many feltmakers prefer this technique of making a nuno-felt jacket because it can be completed in one process. Once the fabric is laid over the template, the fibres put on top and the felting is done it, theoretically, eliminates the need for any sewing. There may be parts that have slipped a little and will need a stitch or two, once the template has been removed.

Making the template

This template has been calculated with a shrinkage factor of 50 per cent and has therefore been made twice the finished size in each direction. You can adapt it for any jacket you wish to make.

The jacket will have a finished size of approximately 105cm (41in) chest/bust and a length of about 70cm (27½in). You can shorten or lengthen it as you wish and calculate the width to your own design and sizing requirements. It is probably easiest to draw the pattern on paper to begin with and transfer it to plastic foam underlay or bubble-wrap when you are satisfied with the shape.

Below: a template for a nuno-felt jacket.

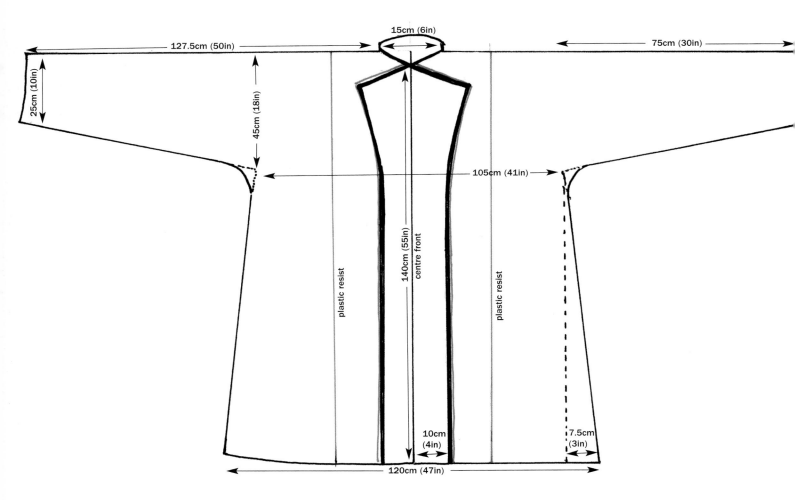

1 Draw a rectangle, the chest measurement x twice the length. In this case it will measure 105 x 140cm (41 x 55in). Draw a line down the centre of the length, which will be the centre front. The top of this line will be the neck. Cut a scoop 4cm (1½in) deep and 7.5cm (3in) across from the centre on each side.

2 Draw the sleeves 75cm (30in) in length and 45cm (18in) down from the shoulder edge, narrowing to 25cm (10in) at the wrist.

3 Add 7.5cm (3in) at the hem to give a small amount of flare, joining the line from the underarm. Curve the line where the sleeve meets the underarm.

4 If you want to have a collar and revers on your jacket, shape the revers now. The front extensions, or wrap will continue down from the revers giving approximately 10cm (4in) on each side. On this jacket the collar is made separately and attached before the final shrinking. This is so that the fabric and wool will appear on the same side as in the body of the coat. Transfer the pattern to your chosen template material. Mark in the revers and front wrap, as shown.

5 Cut a 40 x 140cm (16 x 55in) strip of thin plastic to use as a resist. Place this over the markings on the template and trace the front extensions again.

Right: this jacket was made using a template, with hand-dyed silk fabrics placed on the surface of hand-dyed fibres.

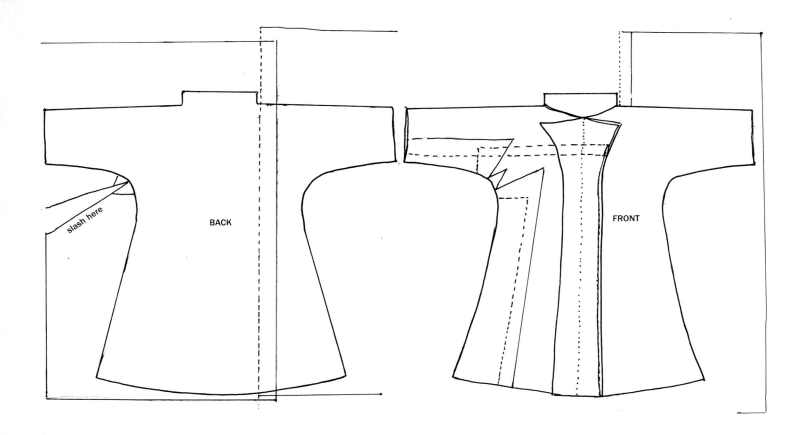

Making the jacket

You will need enough fabric to completely cover your template on both sides. Put the template on top of the bubble-wrap on your prepared table. The first side to be covered will be the back. Lay out your fabric on the template, so that it extends to the bottom of the sleeves. The fabric will not be wide enough to reach from wrist to wrist, but by overlapping separate pieces you will be able to patch and cover it all. You can use different qualities of fabric on the same garment to give greater texture. Chiffon and habotai react with the wool in contrasting ways. The chiffon will merge with wool and appear to be flat and smooth, while the heavier silk will give a much scrunchier texture. You may also like to add some small amounts of a printed fabric.

If you allow a generous overlap there will be less likelihood of the fabric slipping and having to be stitched at a later stage. However, if two layers of thicker fabrics, such as habotai, are overlapping it may be difficult for the wool fibres to migrate through them both, and they will pull apart. Selvedges can make an interesting texture on the surface of the silk, but it is difficult for the wool fibres to work through them. I would advise stitching them and also, if you have lots of separate pieces, you may like to hold them together with a few tacking stitches.

1 Wet the fabric to keep it in place on the template. This will also stop the overlapped fabrics from moving.
2 Slash the fabric under the arms so that you will be able to fold it over the template at a later stage. You will also need to cut around the neck edge, but as this is to be the back of the garment, cut only so that the fabric will easily go round the neck.

Opposite: detail of jacket showing the different textures that can be made by silk fabrics during the shrinking process.

3 Cover the fabric with wool tops and wet with cool, soapy water. Cover the garment with thin plastic and press down well to spread the water and exclude the air. Water the surface of the plastic to help with this. It is likely that you will have to work on the template in sections as it will be quite a huge size, but the plastic will anchor it and allow it to be moved and folded without disturbing the fibres. The sleeves may be left uncovered with wool until you have completed the front sections.

4 Roll the template, fabric and wool up, using a long dowel or plastic foam pipe and turn it over so that the front part of the template is on top and the fabric and wool underneath. Carefully fold the fabric over the template so that it is against the edges, giving a neat edge. Continue to cover one half of this side, trimming the fabric up to the front extension. Wet the fabric to hold it in place. Cover with wool fibres and wet out. Place the thin plastic resist you made with the template, over the front extension matching up the markings. Repeat this process with the other side of the front, cutting the fabric up to the front extension as before. Lay this side with wool fibres, wet and cover the complete front with thin plastic. If you have not yet covered the sleeves then they can now be folded over the body of the garment and covered on both sides. They can be left folded during the rolling. It is important that all the fibres are thoroughly wet before rolling is begun.

5 Roll up the jacket as tightly as possible in bubble-wrap, or for extra friction a matchstick bamboo blind, using whatever roller you have available that is long enough. Put ties around the ends of the bundle to stop any slipping during this process. Roll about 100 times, unroll and turn the felt 90 degrees and roll again. Repeat this until you have rolled in each direction once more. Inspect the felt and make sure that the wool has migrated through the fabric and begun to shrink. Remove the roller but continue to manipulate the jacket and gently drop it on to the table, still in the plastic. Check that there are no holes between the joined fabrics. Repair any gaps with small stitches, which will disappear when the jacket has been fully shrunk.

Collar

Cut a collar 90cm long x 20cm wide (36 x 8in) from the fabrics you have used on the jacket, overlapping and joining where necessary. Cover with wool fibres and felt until the wool is beginning to go through the fabric. Stitch the collar to the jacket, making sure that, when the collar is worn, both fabric sides will be uppermost, or both wool sides. Cover the join with wool fibres so that the seam will disappear when shrunk; work the wool well.

Finishing

Now that the jacket is all in one piece, there are no holes, and the wool is through the fabric, start the shrinking process by rubbing sections of the fabric against the bubble-wrap. Continue with this stage, gradually adding hot water, and keeping the garment soapy, until it has shrunk to the planned size.

Rinse the jacket well in cool water to remove all the soap, squeeze or spin to remove the excess water, re-shape and leave to dry flat.

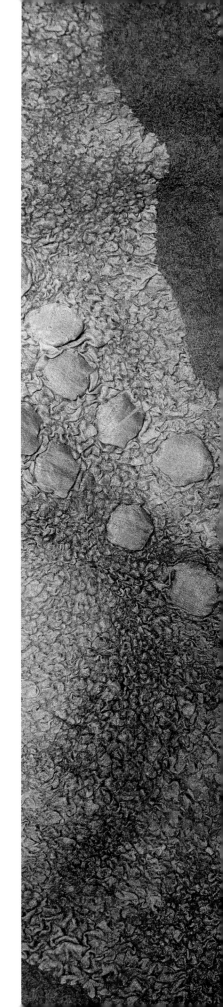

Mosaic jacket

I call this a mosaic jacket because many pieces were fitted together to make the base fabric. A selection of about eight different colours of silk chiffons was made, totalling about 5m (5yd) in length, depending on the required size of the finished jacket. First cut or torn into different widths, they were then re-assembled by stitching. They were then cut again to make squares and rectangles and stitched together until the fabric was the size for making a nuno-felt jacket. Make sure that all the seams are on the same side of the fabric. The seams should be very narrow, or cut narrow after stitching, and pressed flat. The sleeves were cut to shape. This is a very time-consuming method, but the resulting mosaic of colour is worth the effort, I think.

A pallet of wool colours was chosen to complement the colours of the chiffon. Each section of chiffon has a different pattern of wool arranged in it using a contrasting colour. You may like to work out a few simple ideas on paper first, as it is more effective to keep similar designs away from each other (see figure 1, below). Varying the scale can sometimes be all that's needed. The wool was laid with the seams uppermost and, after laying wool inside the rectangles, the seams were covered with wool too. When all the wool has been arranged it can look like a glorious painting.

Complete the garment following the instructions for a nuno-felt jacket (see pages 112–113).

Opposite: detail of mosaic jacket shown on previous page. This detail demonstrates how a different wool pattern is used in each section of the chiffon base fabric.

Figure 1: lay the wool in different patterns in each section.

Above: the jacket has a tie neck,
which has been made with a long
thin strip for a collar.

Right: the edges of the jacket have been left very organic, but are well finished.

Long and full-skirted
nuno-felt coat

This project requires a very large amount of space to work in. It does require a certain amount of sewing skill, as there are several godets to be stitched in. Although it is made in pieces to begin with, when the final shrinking takes place it will be in one piece. The coat is made with a shrinkage factor of 50 per cent; therefore it is made twice as long and twice as wide as the finished size.

The longest pieces of fabric measure 2.5m (2¾yd) long, and the back and front are cut separately and joined later with a shoulder seam.

It can be made using silk or viscose chiffon or georgette. If cotton voile is used it will add more weight and give movement to the full skirt. Velvet and silk organza have been used to embellish this coat. Depending on the base fabric to be used and the width of it, it can take between 12 and 15m (15 and 19yd). The size is for a 90–95cm (35–37in) bust measurement but the sizing can be adapted.

Right: the long skirt of a very flared coat gives weight and fluidity when moving. It is wonderful to wear.

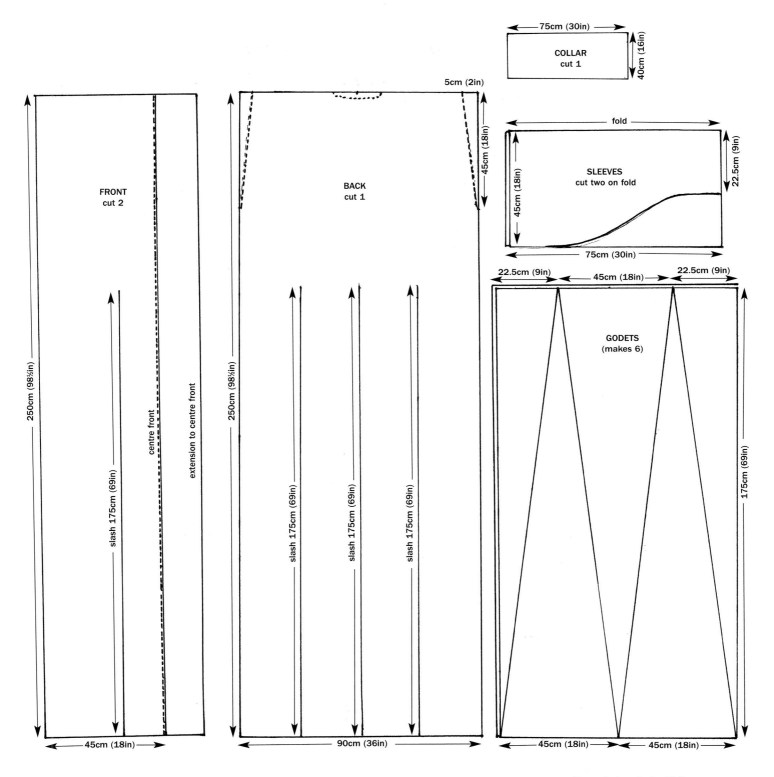

COLLAR
cut 1

75cm (30in)

40cm (16in)

FRONT
cut 2

250cm (98⅜in)

slash 175cm (69in)

centre front

extension to centre front

45cm (18in)

5cm (2in)

BACK
cut 1

45cm (18in)

250cm (98⅜in)

slash 175cm (69in)

slash 175cm (69in)

slash 175cm (69in)

90cm (36in)

fold

SLEEVES
cut two on fold

45cm (18in)

22.5cm (9in)

75cm (30in)

22.5cm (9in)

45cm (18in)

22.5cm (9in)

GODETS
(makes 6)

175cm (69in)

45cm (18in)

45cm (18in)

Above: diagram for long full-
skirted coat using 90cm (36in)
width base fabric. There can be
some flexibility when using a
wider fabric, but try to keep the
same shoulder measurements.

This pattern is based on using a 90cm (36in) wide fabric. A wider cloth can be cut without the front extensions. The coat has three godets in the back, one either side of the front and also in the side seams, totalling seven. The diagram on page 123 shows how to cut six complete godets and there are four half godets too. A pair of these may be used in a side seam.

1 Cut the fabric using the diagram on page 123 as your guide and attach the front extensions if need be, with the narrow seams on the surface and pressed flat. Mark the centre-back neck edge with a very small snip and the centre of the top of the sleeve. Lay the wool on all the pattern pieces, covering the front seam, and add any embellishment. Begin the felting process and work the wool through the fabric to the pre-felt stage.

2 Dry the pieces and press with an iron, trimming away any excess wool that overhangs the edges.

3 Stitch the godets into the slits first. The godet may seem to be longer than the slit. This is because the slit will be on the straight grain of the fabric and the godet slightly on the cross grain, which stretches. Pin the top and bottom of the godet into the slit and ease the rest in, slightly stretching the straight of the fabric. Stitch one side at a time if you are not confident, making a tiny seam. Any imperfections will disappear with the felting and shrinking, especially at the top point.

4 After attaching the godets, join the shoulder seams. Match the snips at the top of the sleeves to the shoulder seam and stitch the sleeves to the body of the coat. Press all the seams flat at this stage. Starting at the wrist, stitch along the underarms and down the sides to the hem. Press these seams flat too. Attach the collar, matching the centre of the collar to the centre-back marking.

5 Working on a section at a time, cover the seams with wool fibres, wet and felt well. As each section is wet and worked, cover with plastic sheeting. Place plastic inside the coat and down the sleeves to prevent both sides felting together. When the complete garment is wet and both sides are covered with plastic the sleeves and skirt may be carefully folded over the body of the coat.

6 Roll the coat up in the bubble-wrap. The wet wool will be very heavy so use a plastic foam roller, if possible, which will not add any extra weight as it is very light. Tie the ends and middle of the roll to prevent it coming undone during the rolling process. Get rid of any water that may be escaping, but do not squeeze too hard as the wool needs to be wet to felt.

7 Follow the rolling procedure as explained on page 91 and complete. Do not forget to stretch and shape the finished garment before rinsing and drying.

Opposite: detail of long coat, showing embellishment with embedded velvets and silk fabrics.

Below: stitch the godets into the slits, attaching the half godets to the side seams.

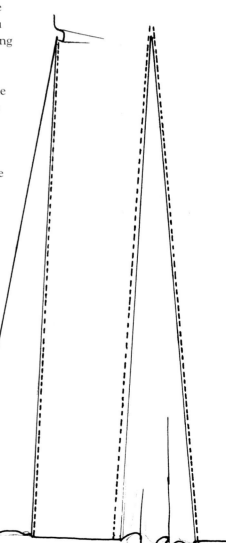

Suppliers

International Feltmakers Association
www.feltmakers.com

Fibres

Handweavers Studio & Gallery Ltd
29 Haroldstone Road
London E17 7AN
tel: 020 8521 2281
www.handweaversstudio.co.uk

Wingham Wool Work
70 Main Street
Wentworth
Rotherham
South Yorkshire S62 7TN
tel: 01226 742 926

Adelaide Walker
Bays 55/56 Pegholms
Wharfedale Business Centre
Otley Mills, Ilkley Road
Otley
West Yorkshire LS21 3JP
tel: 01943 850 812

craftynotions.com
Unit 2, Jessop Way
Newark NG24 2ER
tel: 01636 659 890
www.craftynotions.com

Fibrecrafts
Old Portsmouth Road
Peasmarsh
Guildford
Surrey GU3 1LZ
tel: 01483 565 800
www.fibrecrafts.com

Kartehuset
Vesterskovvej8
DK-5792 Aarslev
Fyn
Denmark
tel: (+45) 65991 919
www.kartehuset.com

Fabrics

Whaleys (Bradford) Ltd
Harris Court
Great Horton Road
Bradford BD7 4EQ
tel: 01274 576 718
www.whaleys-bradford.ltd.uk

Pongees
28–30 Hoxton Square
London N1 6NN
tel: 020 7739 9130

Silk fabrics, fabric paint and embroidery thread

Rainbow Silks
85 High Street
Great Missenden
Buckinghamshire HP16 0AL
tel: 01494 862 111
www.rainbowsilks.co.uk

Fabric paints and dyes

Art Van Go
The Studios
1 Stevenage Road
Knebworth
Hertfordshire SG3 6AN
tel: 01438 814 946
www.artvango.co.uk

Gaywool Dyes
The Threshing Barn
Lower Lady Meadows Farm
Nr Bradnop
Leek
Staffordshire ST13 7EZ
www.threshingbarn.com

Kemtex Colours
Chorley Business and
    Technology Centre
Euxton Lane
Chorley
Lancashire PR7 6TE
tel: 01257 230 220

Omega Dyes
3–5 Regent Street
Stonehouse
Gloucestershire GL10 2AA
tel: 01453 823 691
www.omegadyes.com

Right: nuno-felt jacket by Sue Johnson, constructed using hand-dyed merino needle felt and silk. The jacket is reversible.

Index